Between Faith And Fury

The Story of Hamas

Tariq Nassar

To Lasting Peace

Contents

Introduction

In the heart of the Middle East, a land steeped in ancient history and modern turmoil, the Israeli-Palestinian conflict rages on, fueled by a cycle of violence and yearning for peace. Among the key players in this enduring conflict is Hamas, an entity that defies simple categorization, straddling the line between militant / terror group and political party, between providers of social welfare and proponents of armed struggle and terrorism.

Between Faith and Fury: The Story of Hamas endeavors to unravel the complex tapestry of this Islamist movement that has, since its inception, been a significant and controversial force in Palestinian politics and society. Born from the ashes of the First Intifada in 1987, Hamas emerged as an offshoot of the Muslim Brotherhood, deeply rooted in Islamic ideology and nationalistic fervor. Its name—an acronym for "Islamic Resistance Movement" and an Arabic word for zeal—encapsulates the impassioned ethos driving its mission: the liberation of Palestine through resistance.

This book embarks on a chronological journey, tracing the origins of Hamas amidst the turbulent politics of resistance, exploring its evolving tactics, from suicide bombings to governance, and unraveling its complex relationship with the Palestine Liberation Organization (PLO), Israel, and the broader geopolitical landscape.

As we delve into the ideological underpinnings and the strategic shifts of Hamas, we confront the paradoxes that define it. We see a movement that is at once militant and pragmatic, religiously conservative yet politically adaptable, reviled by many yet undeniably central to the Palestinian cause. We explore the duality of Hamas' identity through its social services—schools, hospitals, and charities—a softer power that has garnered grassroots support, and its military wing, the Izz ad-Din al-Qassam Brigades, which has orchestrated attacks in the name of liberation.

Through the pages of this book, we engage with the voices of Hamas leaders and foot soldiers, of ordinary Palestinians, of Israeli citizens, and of international observers, to gain a multifaceted perspective on the movement's role within the larger narrative of the conflict.

Between Faith and Fury does not aim to champion or chastise, but to illuminate the shades of gray that so often get lost in the black and white portrayal of the conflict. As we turn each page, we seek to understand the motivations that drive Hamas, the realities that shape it, and the future it envisions for Palestine. We look beyond the dichotomy of good and evil, to understand the humanity and the history behind the headlines, to present a narrative as complex and contested as the land for which Hamas stands.

As this book unfolds, so too do the layers of Hamas' story, inviting readers to step into a world where faith and fury intertwine, where the quest for sovereignty collides with the reality of occupation, and where the path to peace remains elusive and steeped in struggle.

Chapter 1

The Formation of Palestinian National Identity

Early history and demographics of the region:

Following the Iron Age, the region experienced the Babylonian conquest, which significantly affected population centers such as Jerusalem, the Shephelah, and the Negev, while the northern Judean and Benjamin areas maintained a demographic continuity. The Edomites settled in southern Judea, and with the fall of the Edomite kingdom, their traditions persisted in the south, later controlled by the Arabic-speaking Qedarites. Along the coast, the Phoenician influence grew, and the hinterlands saw demographic shifts with Moabite and Ammonite refugees settling in, alongside a significant Edomite presence in the southern Judean hills.

The Hellenistic period, ushered in by Alexander the Great's conquests, saw the region of Idumea, linking to the Iron Age kingdom of Edom, encompassing the Arad and Beersheba valleys and the southern Shephelah. The Hellenization process led to the Maccabean Revolt as the Jewish population sought to resist cultural assimilation. By the end of the Hasmonean dynasty, there was a substantial Jewish population, with notable Samaritan communities in Samaria.

The arrival of the Romans in 63 BC began a new era, ending Jewish sovereignty with the fall of the Hasmonean kingdom. The Herodian age, the emergence of Christianity, the Jewish–Roman Wars, and the consequential destruction of the Second Temple in Jerusalem were significant events that reshaped the region's demographics. The Pharisees, precursors to Rabbinic Judaism, numbered around 6,000 at this time. The Roman suppression of revolts led to the dispersal of the Jews from Jerusalem, with many moving to Yavneh on the Mediterranean coast, and others dispersing throughout the Roman Empire.

Following the devastation of Jerusalem, the Romans established a permanent military presence in the city and raised the governor's status, indicating an increase in the region's importance within the empire. Caesarea Maritima became the governor's seat and was graced with the status of a Roman colony. Meanwhile, the Romans founded a new city, Neapolis, as a gesture of gratitude toward the Greeks for their support during the Jewish revolt.

Jewish life recentered around the rabbinical school of Jamnia following the destruction of the Second Temple. Yet, further revolts in the 2nd century, particularly the Bar Kokhba Revolt, led to a dramatic restructuring of the population. In its wake, the province was renamed Syria Palaestina, and Jerusalem was transformed into a Roman city complete with Greco-Roman architecture and cultural institutions. Despite prohibitions against Jewish residency in Jerusalem, evidence suggests that the Jewish presence persisted in the city and remained strong in Galilee, where Tiberias became a new center of Jewish learning and culture. The rural and urban landscapes continued to evolve under Roman influence, with new cities being founded and others being enhanced to reflect the prevailing Greco-Roman culture, marking a period of significant cultural and demographic transformation in the region.

The seventh century ushered in a period of dramatic change for the region of Palestine. The long-standing rivalry between the Byzantine Empire and the Sassanid Empire culminated in several critical battles, with each empire seeking dominance. The Jewish population, caught between these superpowers, experienced shifts in status and autonomy.

In 614, Persian forces captured Jerusalem, which brought a brief period of Persian rule to the city. However, this was not to last. By 627, the Byzantines, led by Emperor Heraclius, regained control after a decisive victory, restoring Christian relics and rule.

The Byzantine resurgence, however, was short-lived. The rise of a new power, the Arabs, brought a fresh wave of change. By 636, Arab forces had vanquished the Byzantine army and by 638, they had taken Jerusalem, beginning a new chapter of Islamic governance that would shape the cultural and religious landscape of the region for the following centuries. The local Jewish communities, while largely powerless during these grand political shifts, held onto hope for a future restoration, a sentiment echoed in their religious hymns and liturgy.

The era following the early Islamic conquests saw Palestine governed by a succession of Islamic caliphates, each leaving its mark on the region's religious and cultural landscape. As the birthplace of Judaism and Christianity, Palestine's strategic location made it a magnet for empires and a focal point for the faithful.

The Umayyad and Abbasid dynasties, among others, presided over an age of architectural and scholarly achievements. The arrival of the Crusaders disrupted Muslim rule, but only temporarily, as Islamic dynasties like the Ayyubids soon restored their control. The region later fell under the sway of the Mamluks, before the Ottoman Turks annexed it, integrating Palestine into their empire for several centuries.

* * *

The Impact of World War I and the Balfour Declaration:

In the early 20th century, following the end of World War I, the United Kingdom was assigned by the League of Nations the task of administering the territories of Palestine and Transjordan, which were previously under the control of the Ottoman Empire. The mandate, which began in 1922, aimed to prepare these areas for eventual self-rule. It included the Balfour Declaration from 1917, committing Britain to the creation of a Jewish homeland in Palestine while also assuring that the rights of the Arab inhabitants would be protected.

Under this mandate, Britain was responsible for managing Jewish immigration, which was a contentious issue that contributed to rising tensions between the Arab and Jewish communities living there. This tension escalated over the years, eventually leading to violent conflicts.

ZIONIST REJOICINGS.

BRITISH MANDATE FOR PALESTINE WELCOMED.

News of the conferment of the mandate for Palestine on Great Britain has created a great impression on Zionist and Jewish circles. A prominent Zionist has given the following views to a representative of the London Jewish Correspondence Bureau :—

The news that Great Britain is to have the mandate for Palestine, and the decision to incorporate the Balfour Declaration in the Treaty of Peace with Turkey will be received with intense gratification by Jews in all countries. It means that at last, after 20 centuries, the Jews will begin the work of re-establishing their ancient Homeland, under a stable and civilized Government. The Wandering Jews will at last have a home.

The Jews have always desired to be under British trusteeship, realizing that the British colonizing methods are based upon the notion of giving free scope to the peoples under British protection. The Zionist leaders at San Remo who have been the spokesmen of the Jewish claims are Dr. Weizmann and Mr. Sokolow. They have been greatly assisted by the support of Mr. Herbert Samuel in this country and of Mr. Justice Brandeis in America.

Another factor which undoubtedly contributed to the granting of the Zionist demands is their great moderation.

The practical consequence of the decision at San Remo will be that Jewish energy and capital will begin to flow towards Palestine to be devoted to the development of the country and to the benefit of all its inhabitants.

The event will be celebrated in all Jewish centres with great joy, and the date—April 24, 1920—will perhaps become a Jewish national holiday. A Zionist Congress, and possibly a Pan-Jewish Congress, will have to be convoked at an early date to concentrate Jewish effort on the restoration of Palestine.—Reuter.

The Times, Monday,
Apr 26, 1920

* * *

The 1936–1939 Arab revolt in Palestine:

The Arab Revolt in Palestine from 1936 to 1939 was a nationalist uprising by Palestinian Arabs against British colonial rule and mass Jewish immigration to the region. The revolt was prompted by growing Arab discontent with the British Mandate authorities and fears of the rising number of Jewish immigrants, which Palestinians perceived as a direct threat to their own national aspirations.

This period of unrest began with a general strike in Jaffa in April 1936, which quickly spread throughout Arab towns and villages. The strike was called by the newly formed Arab Higher Committee, headed by Haj Amin al-Husseini, the Grand Mufti of Jerusalem, and was part of a broader non-violent protest that included a boycott of British goods and refusal to pay taxes.

As the strike prolonged, the revolt evolved into a violent insurrection. Arab bands attacked both British forces and Jewish communities, leading to a series of retaliatory actions by the British and Jewish paramilitary groups. The British responded with martial law, demolishing homes, and conducting widespread arrests to suppress the rebellion. The Jewish community, through organizations such as the Haganah, also mobilized to protect Jewish settlements and retaliate against Arab attacks.

The British government, seeking to quell the uprising, dispatched a commission led by Lord Peel to investigate the causes of the revolt and propose solutions. The Peel Commission concluded that the Mandate was unworkable and recommended partitioning the land into separate

Jewish and Arab states, a proposal that was ultimately rejected by both sides.

By the time the revolt ended in 1939, thousands had been killed, and the Palestinian Arab social and political structure had suffered severe damage. British policy shifted as a result of the revolt and the subsequent White Paper of 1939 limited Jewish immigration and land purchases, aiming to establish an independent Palestinian state within ten years—a promise that was never fulfilled due to the outbreak of World War II and the post-war developments in the region.

The Impact of World War 2 and the Fallout From the Jewish Holocaust:

The end of the British Mandate for Palestine was a complex period that was heavily influenced by the events of World War II and the Holocaust. During the war, the British restricted Jewish immigration to Palestine, a policy that was met with opposition from Jewish groups, particularly as the full horrors of the Holocaust began to emerge. The extermination of six million Jews by Nazi

Germany underscored the desperation and urgency of the Jewish refugee crisis and the Zionist movement's demand for a Jewish state where survivors could find refuge.

After the war, the British continued to face violent resistance from both Jewish and Arab communities in Palestine. Jewish underground organizations, such as the Haganah, Irgun, and Lehi, intensified their campaign against British rule, demanding the opening of Palestine to Jewish immigration. At the same time, Arab nationalism was on the rise, leading to further strife. The British, exhausted by the war and unable to find a viable solution to the growing conflict, referred the matter to the United Nations in 1947.

* * *

The UN Partition Plan and the Civil War in Mandatory Palestine:

The UN partition plan, formally known as United Nations General Assembly Resolution 181, was passed on November 29, 1947. It recommended the end of the British Mandate for

Palestine and the partition of the territory into two independent states, one Jewish and one Arab, with a special international regime for the city of Jerusalem, due to its religious significance.

The plan was a response to the complex and conflicting claims to the land by both Jews and Arabs. The Jewish community, through the Jewish Agency, accepted the plan as it provided a legal basis for the establishment of a Jewish state. In contrast, the Arab leaders and the Arab League rejected the partition, arguing that it 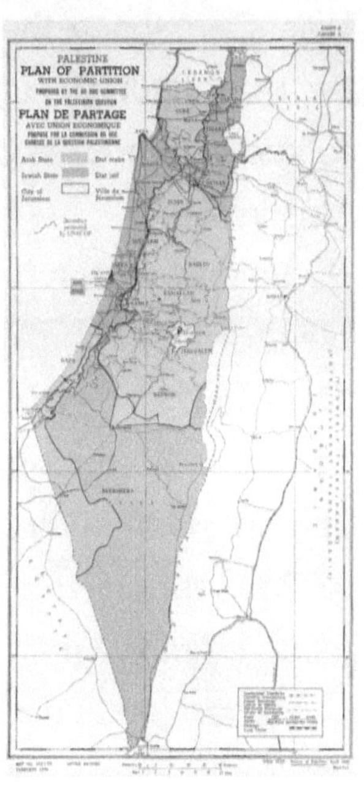 was unfair and that it violated the rights of the majority of the population in Palestine.

The partition plan proposed detailed boundaries for each state and a plan for economic union between them. The Jewish state was to receive about 55% of the land, which included three main areas: the coastal plains, the Galilee, and the Negev desert. The Arab state was allocated about 42% of the land, consisting of the western Galilee, the mountainous region of Judea and Samaria (now commonly referred to as the West Bank), and the Gaza Strip. Jerusalem was to be placed under international control due to its religious importance to Jews, Christians, and Muslims.

Following the adoption of the UN partition plan, civil war broke out in Mandatory Palestine. The conflict was fought between the Jewish community, supported by the Haganah and other Jewish paramilitary groups, and the Palestinian Arabs, supported by the Arab Liberation Army and local Arab militias. The hostilities were characterized by a series of escalating confrontations, violent skirmishes, and acts of terrorism, which led to casualties on both sides and the displacement of populations.

The civil war in Palestine lasted until May 14, 1948, when the British Mandate officially ended, and the State of Israel was declared. This declaration was immediately followed by the intervention of neighboring Arab states, marking the transition from a civil

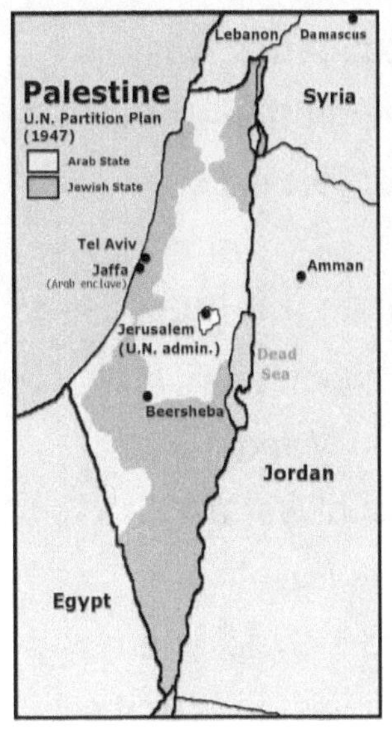

war to a wider regional conflict known as the 1948 Arab-Israeli War.

* * *

1948 Arab-Israeli War:

The 1948 Arab-Israeli War, also known as the War of Independence by Israelis and the Nakba (Catastrophe) by Palestinians, was the first in a series of conflicts in the long-standing Arab-Israeli conflict. It followed the expiration of the British Mandate and the UN's Partition Plan, which the Jewish leadership accepted but the Arab leadership did not.

- **May 14, 1948:** Israel declared its independence as the British Mandate officially ended. The declaration was met with immediate recognition by the United States and the Soviet Union, among others.

- **May 15, 1948:** The conflict transitioned from the civil unrest between Jewish and Arab communities in Mandatory Palestine to a conventional war as neighboring Arab states—Egypt, Transjordan (Jordan), Iraq, Syria, and Lebanon—launched an invasion with the intention of preventing the establishment of a Jewish state and to secure Palestinian Arab sovereignty.
- **Initial Phase:** The Arab forces made initial gains. However, the Israelis managed to halt and then reverse the Arab advance.
- **First Truce:** A UN-mediated ceasefire in June 1948 brought a temporary halt to the fighting. During the truce, Israel reorganized and trained its forces, acquiring weapons and increasing its manpower.

- **Second Phase:** When the fighting resumed, Israeli forces gained the upper hand, capturing areas designated as part of the Arab state by the UN Partition Plan, including mixed cities like Lydda and Ramle, and initiating operations in the Negev and Galilee.
- **Second Truce and Further Fighting:** Another UN-mediated truce took effect in July 1948, but the war continued sporadically. Israeli forces continued to push back the Arab armies and expand their territory beyond the partition plan's boundaries.
- **Armistice Agreements:** Beginning in February 1949, a series of armistice agreements were signed between Israel and the Arab states involved in the conflict, but no formal peace was established. The armistice lines, particularly the one with Jordan (the Green Line), effectively became the borders of the newly formed state.

* * *

The Nakba and the Palestinian Refugee Crisis:

The Nakba, an Arabic term meaning "catastrophe," refers to the events surrounding the establishment of the State of Israel in 1948 and the subsequent displacement of a large number of Palestinian Arabs. The Nakba is a pivotal moment in Palestinian history and is commemorated annually on May 15, the day after the founding of Israel.

During the 1948 Arab-Israeli War, which erupted after Israel declared independence following the end of the British Mandate, between 700,000 and 900,000 Palestinians fled or were expelled from their homes. The reasons for this mass displacement were multifaceted, including fear of violence, actual hostilities, expulsion orders by Israeli forces, and the psychological impact of certain massacres, such as the one at Deir Yassin.

The war resulted in the demolition of hundreds of Palestinian villages and the taking of significant amounts of land for the new state of Israel. Those Palestinians who became refugees ended up in refugee camps in the West Bank, Gaza Strip, and neighboring Arab countries, such as Jordan, Lebanon, and Syria. For Palestinians, the Nakba symbolizes the loss of their homeland and the beginning of a stateless and often precarious existence.

The Palestinian refugee crisis created by the Nakba has been a persistent issue in Middle Eastern politics. The refugees and their descendants, now numbering in the millions, have often been denied citizenship in host countries, leaving them stateless and with limited rights. The right of return for these refugees remains one of the most challenging and controversial aspects of the Israeli-Palestinian conflict. Many Palestinians hold onto keys and deeds from their original homes and lands as symbols of their desired right of return, which has yet to be resolved in peace negotiations.

* * *

The Founding of the PLO and Its Initial Charter:

The Palestine Liberation Organization (PLO) was founded on May 28, 1964, during a summit in East Jerusalem, which was then under Jordanian rule. The PLO was created by the Arab League as a response to the growing sentiment among Palestinians for national liberation and self-determination, following the events of the Nakba and the establishment of the State of Israel in 1948. The organization aimed to centralize the leadership of various Palestinian factions and represent the Palestinian people both nationally and internationally.

The initial charter of the PLO, known as the Palestinian National Covenant or Charter, laid out the organization's principles, objectives, and strategies. This document declared the establishment of an independent Palestinian state as a paramount goal and advocated for the "liberation" of Palestine through armed struggle. The charter denied the legitimacy of the State of Israel and claimed all of British Mandate Palestine as the territory of this prospective Palestinian state, which included present-day Israel.

The PLO's charter also emphasized the importance of Palestinian Arab identity and the unity of the Palestinian people, regardless of their geographical location. It rejected any solution that would compromise the full territorial claims of the

Palestinians or their right to return to the homes from which they were displaced.

Yasser Arafat

Under the leadership of figures like Yasser Arafat, who became the chairman of the PLO's executive committee in 1969, the PLO gained significant political influence and recognition, becoming the recognized representative of the Palestinian people. The early years of the PLO were marked by guerrilla warfare against Israel, including attacks and raids, which led to its classification as a terrorist organization by the United States and Israel at the time.

* * *

Major Factions Within the PLO and Their Ideologies:

- **Fatah**: The largest and most influential faction within the PLO, founded by

Yasser Arafat. Fatah advocated for Palestinian nationalism and initially pursued armed struggle, but later moved towards negotiations with Israel, leading to the Oslo Accords.

- **Popular Front for the Liberation of Palestine (PFLP)**: A Marxist-Leninist group that rejected negotiations and favored armed struggle against the Israeli occupation.
- **Democratic Front for the Liberation of Palestine (DFLP)**: A Marxist-Leninist and revolutionary socialist organization that emphasized national liberation, combined with the struggle for a democratic society in Palestine.
- **Palestine Liberation Front (PLF)**: A smaller faction within the PLO, known for armed attacks, including the hijacking of the Achille Lauro cruise ship in 1985.
- **Palestinian People's Party (PPP)**: Originally the Palestinian Communist Party, it advocates for a Marxist-Leninist

approach and a bi-national state in Palestine.

- **Palestinian Democratic Union (FIDA)**: A democratic socialist and Marxist party that supports the two-state solution and peaceful coexistence between Israelis and Palestinians.

These factions represent a spectrum of political thought within Palestinian society, from secular nationalism and leftist ideologies to more conservative and religious views.

* * *

The Six-Day War and its Aftermath:

The Six-Day War, fought in June 1967, was a conflict between Israel and the Arab states of Egypt, Syria, and Jordan. Preceded by escalating tensions, Israel launched a preemptive strike against Egypt, leading to a rapid succession of battles that resulted in a decisive Israeli victory.

The aftermath of the war significantly altered the map of the Middle East. Israel captured the

Gaza Strip and the Sinai Peninsula from Egypt, the West Bank and East Jerusalem from Jordan, and the Golan Heights from Syria. The victory expanded Israel's territory and had profound implications for regional politics, leading to increased tension and laying the groundwork for future conflicts. The occupation of these territories also had significant implications for the Palestinian population residing in these areas, contributing to the ongoing Israeli-Palestinian conflict.

The Occupation of Gaza and the West Bank:

Israel's control over the West Bank and Gaza Strip commenced following the Six-Day War of 1967, where it seized these areas from Jordan and Egypt. This takeover initiated a profound transformation in terms of governance, population structure, and the Palestinian inhabitants' everyday life.

From 1949 to 1967, the West Bank was under Jordanian rule and experienced an integration into Jordan's administrative framework. Known historically as Judea and Samaria, the topography of the West Bank features a chain of north-south running limestone hills that slope down towards the Jordan River and the Dead Sea. The availability of water resources has influenced the patterns of land use, with agricultural activities in the region ranging from pastoral grazing and cereal farming to the more intensive cultivation of orchards and vegetables in irrigated zones.

The conflicts of 1948 and 1967 led to widespread displacement of Palestinians. In the aftermath of the 1948 conflict, around 300,000 Palestinians sought refuge in what was then Transjordan, and the war in 1967 resulted in approximately 380,000 Palestinians leaving the West Bank. Post-1967, significant demographic changes were observed, particularly in East Jerusalem where many Palestinians were displaced, making way for Jewish settlers.

Industrial progress in the West Bank was modest during the Jordanian era and continued to be limited after the Israeli occupation, with most development efforts directed toward enhancing transportation networks to facilitate military movements and the distribution of agricultural produce.

The enduring Israeli occupation has remained at the heart of the conflict between Israel and the Palestinians, profoundly influencing economic progress, the Palestinians' autonomy, and their freedom of movement. It remains a pivotal point of contention in peace talks and a topic of significant international concern.

The Years Leading to the First Intifada:
The two decades following the Six-Day War in 1967 up to the start of the First Intifada in 1987 were filled with pivotal developments within the Israeli-Palestinian conflict:

- **Israeli Occupation and Settlement Expansion:** Post-war, Israel assumed military control over the newly captured territories and initiated the construction of Jewish settlements, significantly reshaping the population distribution and physical environment of the West Bank, Gaza, and the Golan Heights.

- **War of Attrition (1967-1970):** A drawn-out confrontation, mainly between Israel and Egypt, occurred along the Suez Canal, characterized by periodic battles and special operations.
- **Yom Kippur War (1973):** In a sudden assault during the Yom Kippur holy day, Egypt and Syria attacked Israel. The ensuing conflict was short-lived, ending with a truce facilitated by the U.S.
- **Camp David Accords (1978):** A historic peace treaty brokered by U.S. President Jimmy Carter between Egypt and Israel led to the withdrawal of Israeli forces from the Sinai Peninsula and established a framework for peace in the region.
- **Lebanon War (1982):** To counteract PLO forces, Israel launched an offensive into Lebanon, resulting in an extended engagement that eventually forced the PLO to relocate its base to Tunis.
- **Political Shifts:** In a significant political move, the PLO proclaimed the creation of an independent State of

Palestine in 1988, and Jordan officially relinquished its claims to the West Bank, endorsing the PLO's sovereignty.

These significant occurrences intensified Palestinian grievances and set the stage for the grassroots uprising known as the First Intifada and the birth of Hamas.

Chapter 2

The First Intifada and the Birth of Hamas

The First Intifada, which means "uprising" in Arabic, was a Palestinian popular uprising against Israeli occupation that started in December 1987 and lasted until the Madrid Conference in 1991, although some consider it to have continued until the signing of the Oslo Accords in 1993.

Origins and Causes:

The origins and causes of the First Intifada are rooted in the prolonged and complex history of the Israeli-Palestinian conflict. Key factors that led to this uprising include:

- **Occupation and Settlements:** The Israeli occupation of the West Bank and Gaza Strip following the Six-Day War in 1967, and the subsequent establishment of Israeli settlements in these areas, created deep-seated resentment among Palestinians. They felt their land was being appropriated and their rights as a nation were denied.

- **Political Frustration:** By the late 1980s, Palestinians had lived under Israeli military rule for two decades with little political or civil rights and no clear path to statehood. Efforts through diplomatic channels had stalled, and there was a growing frustration over the lack of progress toward self-determination.

- **Economic Hardship:** The occupation also imposed significant economic hardships on the Palestinian population. Restrictions on movement, trade, and employment opportunities, coupled with the dependency on the Israeli economy, led to high levels of unemployment and poverty in Palestinian areas.

- **Violent Incidents:** Specific events acted as catalysts for the uprising. Notably, in December 1987, an Israeli truck collided with a car carrying Palestinian workers in the Gaza Strip, killing four of them. This incident was widely perceived by Palestinians as a deliberate attack, though it was officially regarded as an accident.
- **Israeli Military Measures:** The heavy-handed approach of the Israeli Defense Forces (IDF) in dealing with Palestinian protests and civil disobedience, which included curfews, house demolitions, and detentions without trial, further fueled anger and a sense of injustice among Palestinians.
- **Rise of Palestinian Identity:** The years leading up to the Intifada saw a growth in Palestinian national consciousness and political activism, partly influenced by wider geopolitical shifts in the Arab world and global discourse on human rights.

- **Local Organizing:** Grassroots organizing had been strengthening within the West Bank and Gaza, with community leaders, activists, and local committees laying the groundwork for collective action.

These factors combined to create an environment ripe for uprising. The initial protests by Palestinians involved in the Intifada were largely nonviolent, consisting of demonstrations, boycotts, and civil disobedience, but as the uprising continued, it became more violent. The Intifada was a spontaneous, grassroots movement that quickly gained momentum and support across the Palestinian territories, profoundly impacting the dynamics of the Israeli-Palestinian conflict.

＊ ＊ ＊

Characteristics:

The First Intifada was a distinctive uprising due to its grassroots nature, widespread participation, and the forms of resistance used by

Palestinians. Here are some of the key characteristics:

- **Popular Participation:** The Intifada was notable for the involvement of people from all walks of Palestinian society. Men, women, and children participated in various forms of resistance. It was a largely leaderless movement at the start, with local community leaders and activists playing critical roles.
- **Nonviolent Resistance:** The Intifada is often remembered for images of youths throwing stones at Israeli tanks and soldiers. However, much of the resistance was nonviolent, including strikes, boycotts of Israeli goods, refusal to pay taxes, graffiti, and the establishment of underground schools (as regular schools were frequently closed by military orders).
- **Civil Disobedience:** Palestinians engaged in widespread civil disobedience, such as refusing to carry Israeli-issued identity cards, which

challenged the administrative control of the Israeli military authorities.

- **Local Committees:** A network of local committees was formed to manage civil affairs, from education and health to food supply and even makeshift courts, as a form of self-governance and a way to minimize dependence on Israeli administration.

- **Economic Boycotts:** Economic resistance took the form of boycotting Israeli products and labor strikes. Palestinians sought to create an independent economy by promoting self-sufficiency and reducing reliance on the Israeli economy.

- **Political Expression:** Palestinians expressed their national and political aspirations through graffiti and the public display of the Palestinian flag, which was banned by Israeli law at the time.

- **Violence and Confrontation:** While the Intifada started with largely nonviolent means, it became increasingly violent over time. There were instances of Palestinians using firearms, Molotov cocktails, and grenades. Israeli settlers and soldiers were targeted, as were Palestinians accused of collaborating with Israel.

- **Israeli Military Response:** The Israeli Defense Forces (IDF) employed a policy of "force, might, and beatings" to suppress the uprising, as per Yitzhak Rabin's infamous order. This included mass arrests, detention without trial, deportations, house demolitions, curfews, and the use of live ammunition and rubber bullets.

- **International Attention:** The Intifada drew international attention to the Palestinian cause. Media coverage highlighted the asymmetric nature of the conflict, often showing armed Israeli soldiers confronting Palestinian children throwing stones.

- **Political Graffiti and Leaflets:** Graffiti and leaflets became important tools for communication within the Palestinian community, calling for resistance, strikes, and conveying messages of national unity.

The First Intifada was a powerful and multifaceted display of resistance that significantly altered the Palestinian national movement and reshaped international perceptions of the Israeli-Palestinian conflict. It led to a shift in the strategies of both the Palestinian leadership and Israel and set the stage for subsequent negotiations and shifts in policy.

* * *

The PLO's Role:

While the uprising began spontaneously, the PLO, led by Yasser Arafat and based in Tunisia at the time, soon began to influence and direct the Intifada. The United National Leadership of the Uprising, a coalition of local Palestinian leaders, issued directives and communiques to guide the resistance, often aligned with PLO positions.

The Intifada was a mobilizing force for Palestinian national identity, drawing international attention to the Palestinian cause. It also saw the rise of local leadership within the Palestinian territories, and the participation of various segments of society, including women and children.

The conflict resulted in a significant loss of life and injuries. According to various sources, more than a thousand Palestinians were killed by Israeli forces, and many more were injured or detained. Israeli casualties were significantly lower. Human rights organizations condemned both sides for abuses, with Israel criticized for its use of lethal force against largely unarmed protesters, and Palestinians criticized for attacks on civilians and intra-Palestinian violence against alleged collaborators.

The Intifada led to a shift in the geopolitical landscape. It was a catalyst for the 1991 Madrid Conference, which for the first time brought together Israeli, Palestinian, and Arab delegates in a peace process, paving the way for the Oslo Accords. These Accords established the Palestinian National Authority and marked the beginning of a new phase in Israeli-Palestinian relations.

* * *

The Impact on the Palestinian Society:

The First Intifada had a profound impact on Palestinian society in several ways that altered how Palestinian's resisted occupation.

- **Mobilization and Unity:** The Intifada mobilized Palestinians from all walks of life and across different political factions, leading to a sense of unity and shared purpose. It involved not just fighters but also everyday citizens—students, workers, and housewives—who participated in acts of civil disobedience and protest.
- **Emergence of Local Leadership:** With the PLO leadership in exile, the Intifada saw the emergence of new local leadership within the Palestinian territories. This leadership coordinated protests, strikes, and the distribution of leaflets, playing a crucial role in maintaining the momentum of the uprising.

- **Cultural and Educational Changes:**
  The Intifada led to a resurgence in
  Palestinian cultural identity and national
  consciousness. Underground schools
  were established to continue education
  despite frequent closures of universities
  and schools by Israeli authorities. These
  schools, along with other informal
  education sessions and community
  discussions, fostered a deeper
  understanding of Palestinian history and
  culture among the youth.
- **Shift in Women's Roles:** Women
  played a significant role in the Intifada,
  taking part in demonstrations,
  organizing boycotts, and maintaining
  the education of children when schools
  were closed. Their participation in the
  uprising led to a shift in gender roles
  and a greater inclusion of women in the
  public sphere of Palestinian society.
- **Economic Self-Reliance:** The boycott
  of Israeli products and services
  encouraged Palestinians to develop
  alternative systems of self-reliance. This

included promoting local agriculture, establishing underground workshops, and creating parallel institutions to address social needs.

- **Political Consequences:** Politically, the Intifada brought international attention to the Palestinian cause. It also pressured the Palestinian leadership to adopt new strategies, leading to a shift from liberation through armed struggle to a peace process approach, which eventually resulted in the Oslo Accords.
- **Human Rights and International Solidarity:** The Intifada drew international scrutiny to the conditions under Israeli occupation and galvanized international solidarity with the Palestinian cause. Human rights organizations and activists around the world focused on the plight of the Palestinians, leading to increased international advocacy.
- **Entrenchment of Occupation:** In response to the Intifada, Israeli military measures intensified. The occupation

became more entrenched, with increased security measures, checkpoints, and restrictions on movement becoming a permanent fixture of life in the occupied territories.

- **Psychological Impact:** The widespread participation in the Intifada, along with the severe Israeli response, had a deep psychological impact on Palestinian society. The experiences of loss, trauma, and resilience during this period have left lasting marks on the collective Palestinian psyche that can be felt to this day.

The Intifada fundamentally altered the Palestinian social fabric, political landscape, and national identity. It was a catalyst for change, leading to significant shifts in how Palestinians engaged with each other, the Israeli state, and the international community.

Casualties and Human Rights Concerns:

- **Palestinian Casualties:** Over the course of the Intifada, various sources reported that more than a thousand Palestinians were killed by Israeli security forces. The majority of these were civilians, including minors. The methods used by the Israeli Defense Forces (IDF) during confrontations, which sometimes involved live ammunition, rubber bullets, and tear gas, led to a high number of injuries as well.

- **Israeli Casualties:** Israeli casualties were considerably fewer in number but included both military personnel and civilians. Israelis were subject to stoning attacks, homemade explosives, and occasional shootings by Palestinian militants.

- **Human Rights Concerns:** Human rights organizations reported widespread abuses during the Intifada. The Israeli response to the uprisings drew particular criticism for what was seen as disproportionate use of force and collective punishment tactics, such as curfews, house demolitions, and the closure of Palestinian schools and universities to quell the uprising. The "breaking bones" policy, where soldiers were instructed to break the limbs of Palestinian protestors to prevent them from throwing stones, was a particularly controversial tactic. This policy was condemned internationally and is one of the most enduring images of the conflict.

- **Detentions and Torture:** Thousands of Palestinians were detained by Israeli forces, with many held without trial in administrative detention. There were also widespread allegations of torture and ill-treatment of Palestinian detainees, which were substantiated by reports from human rights organizations.
- **Violence within Palestinian Society:** The Intifada also saw instances of intra-Palestinian violence. Alleged collaborators with Israel were often

targeted in what were sometimes brutal attacks, including killings.

- **Children and Youth:** A significant aspect of the Intifada was the involvement of Palestinian children and youths, who were often at the forefront of the protests. Many of them were injured, killed, or detained, raising concerns about the impact of the conflict on young people.

The human rights issues arising from the First Intifada had lasting effects and influenced subsequent Israeli military policy, as well as international perceptions of the Israeli-Palestinian conflict. The repercussions of these events continued to be felt in the region and the wider world, shaping the discourse around the conflict and the quest for peace.

* * *

Political Consequences:

The political consequences of the First Intifada were significant and far-reaching, leading to notable shifts in both Palestinian society and the broader Israeli-Palestinian conflict.

- **Shift in Israeli Politics and Society:** The Intifada prompted a reevaluation within Israel of its policies in the Occupied Territories. The protracted uprising and the international attention it garnered put pressure on the Israeli government, which struggled to manage the security situation and maintain its public image. It revealed the unsustainable nature of the occupation and the need for a political solution, contributing to a shift in Israeli public opinion towards seeking a peace process.

- **Empowerment of Palestinian Society:** The uprising galvanized Palestinian society. It brought together various factions and political parties under a common cause, strengthening the Palestinian national identity. It also empowered a new generation of Palestinian leaders from within the

Occupied Territories, reducing the reliance on the external leadership of the PLO and leading to a more localized leadership structure.

- **Enhanced International Recognition:** The Intifada drew international attention to the plight of Palestinians living under occupation. The images of youths confronting tanks and soldiers with stones became a powerful symbol of resistance and led to increased international sympathy and support for the Palestinian cause.
- **PLO's Political Maneuvering:** In response to the Intifada, the PLO under Yasser Arafat's leadership sought to capitalize on the newfound international attention. The PLO endorsed the uprising and sought to position itself as the legitimate representative of the Palestinian people. In 1988, the PLO declared the independence of the State of Palestine, a move that garnered partial international recognition and

bolstered its status in future negotiations.

- **Madrid Conference and Oslo Accords:** The uprising, demonstrating the need for a political resolution to the conflict, led to the Madrid Conference in 1991, where Israelis and Palestinians engaged in direct negotiations for the first time. This eventually led to the Oslo Accords in 1993, which established the Palestinian National Authority and granted limited self-governance to parts of the West Bank and Gaza Strip.

- **Shift Towards Negotiations:** The Intifada's impact forced both Israeli and Palestinian leaderships to consider negotiations as a viable path forward. The subsequent peace process, while fraught with difficulties and setbacks, represented a significant departure from the previous status quo of outright conflict and occupation.

- **Redefinition of the Conflict:** The First Intifada redefined the Israeli-Palestinian conflict from a regional Arab-Israeli dispute to a more focused conflict between Israelis and Palestinians, highlighting the complexities of the issues of sovereignty, statehood, and human rights.

The First Intifada was a watershed moment in Palestinian national history and in the Israeli-Palestinian conflict, setting in motion a series of events that reshaped the political landscape in the region and the nature of the conflict. It showed the limits of military force in resolving the conflict and highlighted the necessity for a political and diplomatic approach, setting the stage for the peace processes of the 1990s.

The Founding of Hamas:

The First Intifada created an environment that contributed to the founding of Hamas. The movement emerged from the Gaza Strip in 1987 as an offshoot of the Egyptian Muslim Brotherhood, transforming the religious-social organization into a political and militant entity that explicitly focused on the Palestinian national struggle and resistance to Israeli occupation.

* * *

Contextual Factors Leading to the Rise of Hamas:

- **Growing Islamist Influence:** In the years leading up to the First Intifada, there was a notable increase in Islamist activity in the Palestinian territories. This movement was partly a response to the perceived failure of secular Arab nationalism, which had dominated Palestinian politics for decades.

- **Social Services Network:** Hamas built upon a well-established network of social and charitable organizations which had gained significant grassroots support among Palestinians, particularly in the Gaza Strip. These networks provided a foundation for political mobilization and support when Hamas transitioned into a political force.
- **Resistance to Occupation:** The Intifada highlighted the Palestinian desire for an end to Israeli occupation, and Hamas positioned itself as a vanguard of armed resistance, in contrast to the PLO's approach, which included both armed struggle and political engagement.
- **Charter and Ideology:** Hamas published its charter in 1988, articulating its principles and objectives.

The charter rejected the PLO's secular nationalism and proposed an Islamic alternative, calling for the establishment of an Islamic state in all of historic Palestine. *(*We will go deeper in the charter in the next chapter.)*

- **Strategic Opening:** The First Intifada weakened traditional Palestinian leadership structures, allowing emerging movements like Hamas to gain influence. The PLO's external base of operations meant that it had a less immediate presence in the territories compared to Hamas.

The First Intifada provided the conditions for Hamas to emerge as a significant actor within the Palestinian national movement. It established itself as an alternative to the PLO, offering a different vision for the Palestinian struggle, one that combined national liberation with Islamist ideology.

Chapter 3

Ideological Foundations

Hamas's Charter and Its Interpretation:

Hamas's charter, officially called the Covenant of the Islamic Resistance Movement, was issued in August 1988. It outlines the organization's ideologies and goals.

- **Islamic Foundations:** The charter establishes Hamas as a strictly Islamic movement, rooted in the principles of Islam and dedicated to the cause of Islam in Palestine.
- **Rejection of Israel's Right to Exist:** The charter explicitly denies the legitimacy of the State of Israel and

calls for the establishment of an Islamic state in all of historic Palestine, which includes present-day Israel.

- **Armed Struggle:** It advocates armed struggle as the primary means of resistance against the Israeli occupation.
- **Link to Muslim Brotherhood:** The document identifies Hamas as a wing of the Muslim Brotherhood in Palestine, sharing the Brotherhood's broader Islamic goals.

* * *

Interpretations and Criticisms:

- **Anti-Semitic Language:** The charter has been widely criticized for containing anti-Semitic language and for perpetuating conspiracy theories against Jews.
- **Rejection of Peace Processes:** It opposes any peaceful resolution that would involve the recognition of Israel

or compromise on the full territorial claims of Palestine.

- **Calls for Liberation:** The document emphasizes the religious and duty-bound aspect of the struggle against Israeli occupation, framing it as not only a nationalistic endeavor but a religious imperative for Muslims.

Contemporary Views:

In more recent years, Hamas has attempted to distance itself from some of the more controversial aspects of the charter. In 2017, Hamas issued a new political document that, while not formally replacing the 1988 charter, suggests a willingness to accept a Palestinian state along the 1967 borders, which is a significant shift from its original stance. However, the original charter has not been retracted, and its content remains a point of contention and a significant barrier to international engagement and peace negotiations.

The charter, and Hamas itself, are seen by many countries, including Israel, the United

States, and the European Union, as promoting terrorism. These countries and organizations have designated Hamas as a terrorist organization due to its commitment to armed struggle and the perpetration of attacks against civilian targets.

The Charter:

In The Name Of The Most Merciful Allah

"Ye are the best nation that hath been raised up unto mankind: ye command that which is just, and ye forbid that which is unjust, and ye believe in Allah. And if they who have received the scriptures had believed, it had surely been the better for them: there are believers among them, but the greater part of them are transgressors. They shall not hurt you, unless with a slight hurt; and if they fight against you, they shall turn their backs to you, and they shall not be helped. They are smitten with vileness wheresoever they are found; unless they

obtain security by entering into a treaty with Allah, and a treaty with men; and they draw on themselves indignation from Allah, and they are afflicted with poverty. This they suffer, because they disbelieved the signs of Allah, and slew the prophets unjustly; this, because they were rebellious, and transgressed." *(Al-Imran – verses 109111).*

Israel will exist and will continue to exist until Islam will obliterate it, just as it obliterated others before it" *(The Martyr, Imam Hassan alBanna, of blessed memory).*

"The Islamic world is on fire. Each of us should pour some water, no matter how little, to extinguish whatever one can without waiting for the others." *(Sheikh Amjad alZahawi, of blessed memory).*

In The Name Of The Most Merciful Allah

Introduction

Praise be unto Allah, to whom we resort for help, and whose forgiveness, guidance and support we seek; Allah bless the Prophet and grant him salvation, his companions and supporters, and to those who carried out his message and adopted his laws everlasting prayers and salvation as long as the earth and heaven will last. Hereafter:

O People:

Out of the midst of troubles and the sea of suffering, out of the palpitations of faithful hearts and cleansed arms; out of the sense of duty, and in response to Allah's command, the call has gone out rallying people together and making them follow the ways of Allah, leading them to have determined will in order to fulfill their role in life, to overcome all obstacles, and surmount the difficulties on the way. Constant preparation has continued and so has the readiness to sacrifice life and all that is precious for the sake of Allah.

Thus it was that the nucleus (of the movement) was formed and started to pave its way through the tempestuous sea of hopes and expectations, of wishes and yearnings, of troubles and obstacles, of pain and challenges, both inside and outside.

When the idea was ripe, the seed grew and the plant struck root in the soil of reality, away from passing emotions, and hateful haste. The Islamic Resistance Movement emerged to carry out its role through striving for the sake of its Creator, its arms intertwined with those of all the fighters for the liberation of Palestine. The spirits of its fighters meet with the spirits of all the fighters who have sacrificed their lives on the soil of Palestine, ever since it was conquered by the companions of the Prophet, Allah bless him and grant him salvation, and until this day.

This Covenant of the Islamic Resistance Movement (HAMAS), clarifies its picture, reveals its identity, outlines its stand, explains its aims, speaks about its hopes, and calls for its support, adoption and joining its ranks. Our struggle against the Jews is very great and very serious. It needs all sincere efforts. It is a step that inevitably should be *followed by other steps. The Movement is but one squadron that should be supported by more and more squadrons from this vast Arab and Islamic world, until the enemy is vanquished and Allah's victory is realized.*

Thus we see them coming on the horizon "and you shall learn about it hereafter" "Allah hath written, Verily I will prevail, and my apostles: for Allah is strong and mighty." (The Dispute – verse 21).

"Say to them, This is my way: I invite you to Allah, by an evident demonstration; both I and he who followeth me; and, praise be unto Allah! I am not an idolater." (Joseph – verse 107).

Hamas (means) strength and bravery – (according to) Al-Mua'jam al-Wasit: c1.

Definition of the Movement

Ideological Starting-Points

Article One:

The Islamic Resistance Movement: The Movement's program is Islam. From it, it draws its ideas, ways of thinking and understanding of the universe, life and man. It resorts to it for judgement in all its conduct, and it is inspired by it for guidance of its steps.

The Islamic Resistance Movement's Relation With the Muslim Brotherhood Group:

Article Two:

The Islamic Resistance Movement is one of the wings of Muslim Brotherhood in Palestine. Muslim Brotherhood Movement is a universal organization which constitutes the largest Islamic movement in modern times. It is characterized by its deep understanding, accurate comprehension and its complete embrace of all Islamic concepts of all aspects of life, culture, creed, politics, economics, education, society, justice and judgement, the spreading of Islam, education, art, information, science of the occult and conversion to Islam.

Structure and Formation

Article Three:

The basic structure of the Islamic Resistance Movement consists of Muslims who have given their allegiance to Allah whom they truly worship, "I have created the jinn and humans only for the purpose of worshipping" who know their duty towards themselves, their families and country. In all that, they fear Allah and raise the banner of Jihad in the face of the oppressors, so that they would rid the land and the people of their uncleanliness, vileness and evils.

"But we will oppose truth to vanity, and it shall confound the same; and behold, it shall vanish away." (Prophets – verse 18).

Article Four:

The Islamic Resistance Movement welcomes every Muslim who embraces its faith, ideology, follows its program, keeps its secrets, and wants to belong to its ranks and carry out the duty. Allah will certainly reward such one.

Time and Place Extent of the Islamic Resistance Movement:

Article Five:

Time extent of the Islamic Resistance Movement: By adopting Islam as its way of life, the Movement goes back to the time of the birth of the Islamic message, of the righteous ancestor, for Allah is its target, the Prophet is its example and the Koran is its constitution. Its extent in place is anywhere that there are Muslims who embrace Islam as their way of life everywhere in the globe. This being so, it extends to the depth of the earth and reaches out to the heaven.

"Dost thou not see how Allah putteth forth a parable; representing a good word, as a good tree, whose root is firmly fixed in the earth, and whose branches reach unto heaven; which bringeth forth its fruit in all seasons, by the will of its Lord? Allah propoundeth parables unto men, that they may be instructed." (Abraham – verses 24-25).

Characteristics and Independence: Article Six:

The Islamic Resistance Movement is a distinguished Palestinian movement, whose allegiance is to Allah, and whose way of life is Islam. It strives to raise the banner of Allah over every inch of Palestine, for under the wing of Islam followers of all religions can coexist in security and safety where their lives, possessions and rights are concerned. In the absence of Islam, strife will be rife, oppression spreads, evil prevails and schisms and wars will break out.

How excellent was the Muslim poet, Mohamed Ikbal, when he wrote:

"If faith is lost, there is no security and there is no life for him who does not adhere to religion. He who accepts life without religion, has taken annihilation as his companion for life."

The Universality of the Islamic Resistance Movement:

Article Seven:

As a result of the fact that those Muslims who adhere to the ways of the Islamic Resistance Movement spread all over the world, rally support for it and its stands, strive towards enhancing its struggle, the Movement is a universal one. It is well-equipped for that because of the clarity of its ideology, the nobility of its aim and the loftiness of its objectives.

On this basis, the Movement should be viewed and evaluated, and its role be recognized. He who denies its right, evades supporting it and turns a blind eye to facts, whether intentionally or unintentionally, would awaken to see that events have overtaken him and with no logic to justify his attitude. One should certainly learn from past examples.

The injustice of next-of-kin is harder to bear than the smite of the Indian sword.

"We have also sent down unto thee the book of the Koran with truth, confirming that scripture which was revealed before it; and preserving the same safe from corruption. Judge therefore between them according to that which Allah hath revealed; and follow not their desires, by swerving from the truth which hath come unto thee. Unto every of you have we given a law, and an open path; and if Allah had pleased, he had surely made you one people; but he hath thought it fit to give you different laws, that he might try you in that which he hath given you respectively.

Therefore strive to excel each other in good works; unto Allah shall ye all return, and then will he declare unto you that concerning which ye have disagreed." (The Table, verse 48).

The Islamic Resistance Movement is one of the links in the chain of the struggle against the Zionist invaders. It goes back to 1939, to the emergence of the martyr Izz al-Din al Kissam and his brethren the fighters, members of Muslim Brotherhood. It goes on to reach out and become one with another chain that includes the struggle of the Palestinians and Muslim Brotherhood in the 1948 war and the Jihad operations of the Muslim Brotherhood in 1968 and after.

Moreover, if the links have been distant from each other and if obstacles, placed by those who are the lackeys of Zionism in the way of the fighters obstructed the continuation of the struggle, the Islamic Resistance Movement aspires to the realization of Allah's promise, no matter how long that should take. The Prophet,

Allah bless him and grant him salvation, has said:

The Day of Judgement will not come about until Muslims fight the Jews. When the Jew will hide behind stones and trees, the stones and trees will say, "O Muslims, O Abdulla, there is a Jew behind me, come and kill him. Only the Gharkad tree, (evidently a certain kind of tree) would not do that because it is one of the trees of the Jews." (related by al-Bukhari and Muslim).

The Slogan of the Islamic Resistance Movement:

Article Eight:

Allah is its target, the Prophet is its model, the Koran its constitution: Jihad is its path and death for the sake of Allah is the loftiest of its wishes.

Objectives

Incentives and Objectives:

Article Nine:

The Islamic Resistance Movement found itself at a time when Islam has disappeared from life. Thus rules shook, concepts were upset, values changed and evil people took control, oppression and darkness prevailed, cowards became like tigers: homelands were usurped, people were scattered and were caused to wander all over the world, the state of justice disappeared and the state of falsehood replaced it. Nothing remained in its right place. Thus, when Islam is absent from the arena, everything changes. From this state of affairs the incentives are drawn.

As for the objectives: They are the fighting against the false, defeating it and vanquishing it so that justice could prevail, homelands be retrieved and from its mosques would the voice of the muezzin emerge declaring the establishment of the state of Islam, so that people and things would return each to their right places and Allah is our helper.

"...and if Allah had not prevented men, the one by the other, verily the earth had been corrupted: but Allah is beneficent towards his creatures." (The Cow – verse 251).

Article Ten:

As the Islamic Resistance Movement paves its way, it will back the oppressed and support the wronged with all its might. It will spare no effort to bring about justice and defeat injustice, in word and deed, in this place and everywhere it can reach and have influence therein.

Strategies and Methods
Strategies of the Islamic Resistance Movement: Palestine Is Islamic Waqf:
Article Eleven:

The Islamic Resistance Movement believes that the land of Palestine is an Islamic Waqf consecrated for future Muslim generations until Judgement Day. It, or any part of it, should not be squandered: it, or any part of it, should not be given up. Neither a single Arab country nor all Arab countries, neither any king or president, nor all the kings and presidents, neither any organization nor all of them, be they Palestinian or Arab, possess the right to do that. Palestine is an Islamic Waqf land consecrated for Muslim generations until Judgement Day. This being so, who could claim to have the right to represent Muslim generations till Judgement Day?

This is the law governing the land of Palestine in the Islamic Sharia (law) and the same goes for any land the Muslims have conquered by force, because during the times of (Islamic) conquests, the Muslims consecrated these lands to Muslim generations till the Day of Judgement.

It happened like this: When the leaders of the Islamic armies conquered Syria and Iraq, they sent to the Caliph of the Muslims, Umar bin-el-Khatab, asking for his advice concerning the conquered land whether they should divide it among the soldiers, or leave it for its owners, or what? After consultations and discussions between the Caliph of the Muslims, Omar bin-el-Khatab and companions of the Prophet, Allah bless him and grant him salvation, it was decided that the land should be left with its owners who could benefit by its fruit. As for the real ownership of the land and the land itself, it should be consecrated for Muslim generations till Judgement Day. Those who are on the land, are there only to benefit from its fruit. This Waqf remains as long as earth and heaven remain. Any procedure in contradiction to Islamic Sharia, where Palestine is concerned, is null and void.

"Verily, this is a certain truth. Wherefore praise the name of thy Lord, the great Allah." (The Inevitable – verse 95).

Homeland and Nationalism from the Point of View

of the Islamic Resistance Movement in Palestine:

Article Twelve:

Nationalism, from the point of view of the Islamic Resistance Movement, is part of the religious creed. Nothing in nationalism is more significant or deeper than in the case when an enemy should tread Muslim land. Resisting and quelling the enemy become the individual duty of every Muslim, male or female. A woman can go out to fight the enemy without her husband's permission, and so does the slave: without his master's permission.

Nothing of the sort is to be found in any other regime. This is an undisputed fact. If other nationalist movements are connected with materialistic, human or regional causes, nationalism of the Islamic Resistance Movement has all these elements as well as the more important elements that give it soul and life. It is connected to the source of spirit and the granter of life, hoisting in the sky of the homeland the heavenly banner that joins earth and heaven with a strong bond.

If Moses comes and throws his staff, both witch and magic are annulled.

"Now is the right direction manifestly distinguished from deceit: whoever therefore shall deny Tagut, and believe in Allah, he shall surely take hold with a strong handle, which shall not be broken; Allah is he who heareth and seeth." (The Cow – Verse 256).

Peaceful Solutions, Initiatives and International Conferences:

Article Thirteen:

Initiatives, and so-called peaceful

solutions and international conferences, are in contradiction to the principles of the Islamic Resistance Movement. Abusing any part of Palestine is abuse directed against part of religion. Nationalism of the Islamic Resistance Movement is part of its religion. Its members have been fed on that. For the sake of hoisting the banner of Allah over their homeland they fight. "Allah will be prominent, but most people do not know."

Now and then the call goes out for the convening of an international conference to look for ways of solving the (Palestinian) question. Some accept, others reject the idea, for this or other reason, with one stipulation or more for consent to convening the conference and participating in it. Knowing the parties constituting the conference, their past and present attitudes towards Muslim problems, the Islamic Resistance Movement does not consider these conferences capable of realizing the demands, restoring the rights or doing justice to the oppressed. These conferences are only ways of setting the infidels in the land of the Muslims as arbitrators. When did the infidels do justice to the believers?

"But the Jews will not be pleased with thee, neither the Christians, until thou follow their religion; say, The direction of Allah is the true direction. And verily if thou follow their desires, after the knowledge which hath been given thee, thou shalt find no patron or protector against Allah." (The Cow – verse 120).

There is no solution for the Palestinian question except through Jihad. Initiatives, proposals and international conferences are all a waste of time and vain endeavors. The Palestinian people know better than to consent to having their future, rights and fate toyed with. As in said in the honorable Hadith:

"The people of Syria are Allah's lash in His land. He wreaks His vengeance through them against whomsoever He wishes among His slaves It is unthinkable that those who are double-faced among them *should prosper over the faithful. They will certainly die out of grief and desperation."*

The Three Circles:

Article Fourteen:

The question of the liberation of Palestine is bound to three circles: the Palestinian circle, the Arab circle and the Islamic circle. Each of these circles has its role in the struggle against Zionism. Each has its duties, and it is a horrible mistake and a sign of deep ignorance to overlook any of these circles. Palestine is an Islamic land which has the first of the two kiblahs (direction to which Muslims turn in praying), the third of the holy (Islamic) sanctuaries, and the point of departure for Mohamed's midnight journey to the seven heavens (i.e. Jerusalem).

"Praise be unto him who transported his servant by night, from the sacred temple of Mecca to the farther temple of Jerusalem, the circuit of which we have blessed, that we might show him some of our signs; for Allah is he who heareth, and seeth." (The Night Journey – verse 1).

Since this is the case, liberation of Palestine is then an individual duty for very Muslim wherever he may be. On this basis, the problem should be viewed. This should be realized by every Muslim.

The day the problem is dealt with on this basis, when the three circles mobilize their capabilities, the present state of affairs will change and the day of liberation will come nearer.

"Verily ye are stronger than they, by reason of the terror cast into their breasts from Allah. This, because they are not people of prudence." (The Emigration – verse 13).

The Jihad for the Liberation of Palestine is an Individual Duty:

Article Fifteen:

The day that enemies usurp part of Muslim land, Jihad becomes the individual duty of every Muslim. In face of the Jews' usurpation of Palestine, it is compulsory that the banner of Jihad be raised. To do this requires the diffusion of Islamic consciousness among the masses, both on the regional, Arab and Islamic levels. It is necessary to instill the spirit of Jihad in the heart of the nation so that they would confront the enemies and join the ranks of the fighters.

It is necessary that scientists, educators and teachers, information and media people, as well as the educated masses, especially the youth and sheikhs of the Islamic movements, should take part in the operation of awakening (the masses). It is important that basic changes be made in the school curriculum, to cleanse it of the traces of ideological invasion that affected it as a result of the orientalists and missionaries who infiltrated the region following the defeat of the Crusaders at the hands of Salah el-Din (Saladin). The Crusaders realized that it was impossible to defeat the Muslims without first having ideological invasion pave the way by upsetting their thoughts, disfiguring their heritage and violating their ideals. Only then could they invade with soldiers. This, in its turn, paved the way for the imperialistic invasion that made Allenby declare on entering Jerusalem: "Only now have the Crusades ended." General Guru stood at Salah el-Din's grave and said: "We have returned, O Salah el-Din." Imperialism has helped towards the strengthening of ideological invasion, deepening, and still does, its roots. All this has paved the way towards the loss of Palestine.

It is necessary to instill in the minds of the Muslim generations that the Palestinian problem is a religious problem, and should be dealt with on this basis. Palestine contains Islamic holy sites. In it there is al-Aqsa Mosque which is bound to the great Mosque in Mecca in an inseparable bond as long as heaven and earth speak of Isra` (Mohammed's midnight journey to the seven heavens) and Mi'raj (Mohammed's ascension to the seven heavens from Jerusalem).

"The bond of one day for the sake of Allah is better than the world and whatever there is on it. The place of one's whip in Paradise is far better than the world and

whatever there is on it. A worshipper's going and coming in the service of Allah is better than the world and whatever there is on it." (As related by al-Bukhari, Muslim, al-Tarmdhi and Ibn Maja).

"I swear by the holder of Mohammed's soul that I would like to invade and be killed for the sake of Allah, then invade and be killed, and then invade again and be killed." (As related by al-Bukhari and Muslim).

The Education of the Generations:
Article Sixteen:

It is necessary to follow Islamic orientation in educating the Islamic generations in our region by teaching the religious duties, comprehensive study of the Koran, the study of the Prophet's Sunna (his sayings and doings), and learning about Islamic history and heritage from their authentic sources. This should be done by specialized and learned people, using a curriculum that would healthily form the thoughts and faith of the Muslim student. Side by side with this, a comprehensive study of the enemy, his human and financial capabilities, learning about his points of weakness and strength, and getting to know the forces supporting and helping him, should also be included. Also, it is important to be acquainted with the current events, to follow what is new and to study the analysis and commentaries made of these events. Planning for the present and future, studying every trend appearing, is a must so that the fighting Muslim would live knowing his aim, objective and his way in the midst of what is going on around him.

"O my son, verily every matter, whether good or bad, though it be the weight of a grain of mustardseed, and be hidden in a rock, or in the heavens, or in the earth, Allah will bring the same to light; for Allah is clearsighted and knowing. O my son, be constant at prayer, and command that which is just, and forbid that which is evil: and be patient under the afflictions which shall befall thee; for this is a duty absolutely incumbent on all men. Distort *not thy face out of contempt to men, neither walk in the earth with insolence; for Allah loveth no arrogant, vainglorious person." (Lokman – verses 16-18).*

The Role of the Muslim Woman:
Article Seventeen:

The Muslim woman has a role no less important than that of the Muslim man in the battle of liberation. She is the maker of men. Her role in guiding and educating the new generations is great. The enemies have realized the importance of her role. They consider that if they are able to direct and bring her up the way they wish, far from Islam, they would have won the battle. That is why you find them giving these attempts constant attention through information campaigns, films, and the school curriculum, using for that purpose their lackeys who are infiltrated through Zionist organizations under various names and shapes, such as Freemasons, Rotary Clubs, espionage groups and others, which are all nothing more than cells of subversion and saboteurs. These organizations have ample resources that enable them to play their role in societies for the purpose of achieving the Zionist targets and to deepen the concepts that would serve the enemy. These organizations operate in the absence of Islam and its estrangement among its people. The Islamic peoples should perform their role in confronting the conspiracies of these saboteurs. The day Islam is in control of guiding the affairs of life, these organizations, hostile to humanity and Islam, will be obliterated.

Article Eighteen:

Woman in the home of the fighting family, whether she is a mother or a sister, plays the most important role in looking after the family, rearing the children and imbuing them with moral values and thoughts derived from Islam. She has to teach them to perform the religious duties in preparation for the role of fighting awaiting them. That is why it is necessary to pay great attention to schools and the curriculum followed in educating Muslim girls, so that they would grow up to be good *mothers, aware of their role in the battle of liberation.*

She has to be of sufficient knowledge and understanding where the performance of housekeeping matters is concerned, because economy and avoidance of waste of the family budget, is one of the requirements for the ability to continue moving forward in the difficult conditions surrounding us. She should put before her eyes the fact that the money available to her is just like blood which should never flow except through the veins so that both children and grownups could continue to live.

"Verily, the Muslims of either sex, and the true believers of either sex, and the devout men, and the devout women, and the men of veracity, and the women of veracity, and the patient men, and the patient women, and the humble men, and the humble women, and the almsgivers of either sex who remember Allah frequently; for them hath Allah prepared forgiveness

and a great reward." (The Confederates – verse 25).

The Role of Islamic Art in the Battle of Liberation:

Article Nineteen:

Art has regulations and measures by which it can be determined whether it is Islamic or pre-Islamic (Jahili) art. The issues of Islamic liberation are in need of Islamic art that would take the spirit high, without raising one side of human nature above the other, but rather raise all of them harmoniously an in equilibrium.

Man is a unique and wonderful creature, made out of a handful of clay and a breath from Allah. Islamic art addresses man on this basis, while pre-Islamic art addresses the body giving preference to the clay component in it.

The book, the article, the bulletin, the sermon, the thesis, the popular poem, the poetic ode, the song, the play and others, contain the characteristics of Islamic art, then these are among the requirements of ideological mobilization, renewed food for the journey and recreation for the soul. The road is long and suffering is plenty. The soul will be bored, but Islamic art renews the energies, resurrects the movement, arousing in them lofty meanings and proper conduct. "Nothing can improve the self if it is in retreat except shifting from one mood to another."

All this is utterly serious and no jest, for those who are fighters do not jest.

Social Mutual Responsibility:
Article Twenty:

Muslim society is a mutually responsible society. The Prophet, prayers and greetings be unto him, said: "Blessed are the generous, whether they were in town or on a journey, who have collected all that they had and shared it equally among themselves."

The Islamic spirit is what should prevail in every Muslim society. The society that confronts a vicious enemy which acts in a way similar to Nazism, making no differentiation between man and woman, between children and old people – such a society is entitled to this Islamic spirit. Our enemy relies on the methods of collective punishment. He has deprived people of their homeland and properties, pursued them in their places of exile and gathering, breaking bones, shooting at women, children and old people, with or without a reason. The enemy has opened detention camps where thousands and thousands of people are thrown and kept under sub-human conditions. Added to this, are the demolition of houses, rendering children orphans, meting cruel sentences against thousands of young people, and causing them to spend the best years of their lives in the dungeons of prisons.

In their Nazi treatment, the Jews made no exception for women or children. Their policy of striking fear in the heart is meant for all. They attack people where their breadwinning is concerned, extorting their money and threatening their honor. They deal with people as if they were the worst war criminals. Deportation from the homeland is a kind of murder.

To counter these deeds, it is necessary that social mutual responsibility should prevail among the people. The enemy should be faced by the people as a single body which if one member of it should complain, the rest of the body would respond by feeling the same pains.

Article Twenty-One:

Mutual social responsibility means extending assistance, financial or moral, to all those who are in need and joining in the execution of some of the work. Members of the Islamic Resistance Movement should consider the interests of the masses as their own personal interests. They must spare no effort in achieving and preserving them. They must prevent any foul play with the future of the upcoming generations and anything that could cause loss to society. The masses are part of them and they are part of the masses. Their strength is theirs, and their future is theirs. Members of the Islamic Resistance Movement should share the people's joy and grief, adopt the demands of the public and whatever means by which they could be realized. The day that such a spirit prevails, brotherliness would deepen, cooperation, sympathy and unity will be enhanced and the ranks will be solidified to confront the enemies.

Supportive Forces Behind the Enemy:

Article Twenty-Two:

For a long time, the enemies have been planning, skillfully and with precision, for the achievement of what they have attained. They took into consideration the causes affecting the current of events. They strived to amass great and substantive material wealth which they devoted to the realizations of their dream. With their money, they took control of the world media, news agencies, the press, publishing houses, broadcasting stations, and others. With their money they stirred revolutions in various parts of the world with the purpose of achieving their interests and reaping the fruit therein. They were behind the French Revolution, the Communist revolution and most of the revolutions we heard and hear *about, here and there. With their money they formed secret societies, such as Freemasons, Rotary Clubs, the Lions and others in different parts of the world for the purpose of sabotaging societies and achieving Zionist interests. With their money they were able to control imperialistic countries and instigate them to colonize many countries in order to enable them to exploit their resources and spread corruption there.*

You may speak as much as you want about regional and world wars. They were behind World War I, when they were able to destroy the Islamic Caliphate, making financial gains and controlling resources. They obtained the Balfour Declaration, formed the League of Nations through which they could rule the world. They were behind World War II, through which they made huge financial gains by trading in armaments, and paved the way for the establishment of their state. It was they who instigated the replacement of the League of Nations with the United Nations and the Security Council to enable them to rule the world through them. There is no war going on anywhere, without having their finger in it.

"So often as they shall kindle a fire for war, Allah shall extinguish it; and they shall set their minds to act corruptly in the earth, but Allah loveth not the corrupt doers." (The Table – verse 64).

The imperialistic forces in the Capitalist West and Communist East, support the enemy with all their might, in money and in men. These forces take turns in doing that. The day Islam appears, the forces of infidelity would unite to challenge it, for the infidels are of one nation.

"O true believers, contract not an intimate friendship with any besides yourselves: they will not fail to corrupt you. They wish for that which may cause you to perish: their hatred hath already appeared from out of their mouths; but what their breasts conceal is yet more inveterate. We have already shown you signs of their ill will

towards you, if ye understand." (The Family of Imran – verse 118).

It is not in vain that the verse is ended with Allah's words "if ye understand."

Our Attitudes Towards:

A. Islamic Movements:

Article Twenty-Three:

The Islamic Resistance Movement views other Islamic movements with respect and appreciation. If it were at variance with them on one point or opinion, it is in agreement with them on other points and understandings. It considers these movements, if they reveal good intentions and dedication to Allah, that they fall into the category of those who are trying hard since they act within the Islamic circle. Each active person has his share.

The Islamic Resistance Movement considers all these movements as a fund for itself. It prays to Allah for guidance and directions for all and it spares no effort to keep the banner of unity raised, ever striving for its realization in accordance with the Koran and the Prophet's directives.

"And cleave all of you unto the covenant of Allah, and depart not from it, and remember the favor of Allah towards you: since ye were enemies, and he reconciled your hearts, and ye became companions and brethren by his favor: and ye were on the brink of a pit of fire, and he delivered you thence. Allah declareth unto you his signs, that ye may be directed." (The Family of Imran – Verse 102).

Article Twenty-Four:

The Islamic Resistance Movement does not allow slandering or speaking ill of individuals or groups, for the believer does not indulge in such malpractices. It is necessary to differentiate between this behavior and the stands taken by certain individuals and groups. Whenever those stands are erroneous, the Islamic Resistance Movement preserves the right to expound the error and to warn against it. It will strive to show the right path and to judge the case in question with objectivity. Wise conduct is indeed the target of the *believer who follows it wherever he discerns it.*

"Allah loveth not the speaking ill of anyone in public, unless he who is injured call for assistance; and Allah heareth and knoweth: whether ye publish a good action, or conceal it, or forgive evil, verily Allah is gracious and powerful." (Women – verses 147148).

B. Nationalist Movements in the Palestinian Arena:

Article Twenty-Five:

The Islamic Resistance Movement respects these movements and appreciates their circumstances and the conditions surrounding and affecting them. It encourages them as long as they do not give their allegiance to the Communist East or the Crusading West. It confirms to all those who are integrated in it, or sympathetic towards it, that the Islamic Resistance Movement is a fighting movement that has a moral and enlightened look of life and the way it should cooperate with the other (movements). It detests opportunism and desires only the good of people, individuals and groups alike. It does not seek material gains, personal fame, nor does it look for a reward from others. It works with its own resources and whatever is at its disposal "and prepare for them whatever force you can," for the fulfilment of the duty, and the earning of Allah's favor. It has no other desire than that.

The Movement assures all the nationalist trends operating in the Palestinian arena for the liberation of Palestine, that it is there for their support and assistance. It will never be more than that, both in words and deeds, now and in the future. It is there to bring together and not to divide, to preserve and not to squander, to unify and not to throw asunder. It evaluates every good word, sincere effort and good offices. It closes the door in the face of side disagreements and does not lend an ear to rumors and slanders, while at the same time fully realizing the right for self-defense.

Anything contrary or contradictory to these trends, is a lie disseminated by enemies or their lackeys for the purpose of sowing confusion, disrupting the ranks and occupy them with side issues.

"O true believers, if a wicked man come unto you with a tale, inquire strictly into the truth thereof; lest ye hurt people through ignorance, and afterwards repent of what ye have done." (The Inner Apartments – verse 6).

Article Twenty-Six:

In viewing the Palestinian nationalist movements that give allegiance neither to the East nor the West, in this positive way, the Islamic Resistance Movement does not refrain from discussing new situations on the regional or international levels where the Palestinian question is concerned. It does that in such an objective manner revealing the extent of how much it is in harmony or contradiction with the national interests in the light of the Islamic point of view.

C. The Palestinian Liberation Organization:

Article Twenty-Seven:

The Palestinian Liberation Organization is the closest to the heart of the Islamic Resistance Movement. It contains the father and the brother, the next of kin and the friend. The Muslim does not estrange himself from his father, brother, next of kin or friend. Our homeland is one, our situation is one, our fate is one and the enemy is a joint enemy to all of us.

Because of the situations surrounding the formation of the Organization, of the ideological confusion prevailing in the Arab world as a result of the ideological invasion under whose influence the Arab world has fallen since the defeat of the Crusaders and which was, and still is, intensified through orientalists, missionaries and imperialists, the Organization adopted the idea of the secular state. And that it how we view it.

Secularism completely contradicts religious ideology. Attitudes, conduct and decisions stem from ideologies.

That is why, with all our appreciation for The Palestinian Liberation Organization - and what it can develop into and without belittling its role in the Arab-Israeli conflict, we are unable to exchange the present or future Islamic Palestine with the secular idea. The Islamic nature of Palestine is part of our religion and whoever takes his religion lightly is a loser.

"Who will be adverse to the religion of Abraham, but he whose mind is infatuated? (The Cow – verse 130).

The day The Palestinian Liberation Organization adopts Islam as its way of life, we will become its soldiers, and fuel for its fire that will burn the enemies.

Until such a day, and we pray to Allah that it will be soon, the Islamic Resistance Movement's stand towards the PLO is that of the son towards his father, the brother towards his brother, and the relative to relative, suffers his pain and supports him in confronting the enemies, wishing him to be wise and well-guided.

"Stand by your brother, for he who is

brotherless is like the fighter who goes to battle without arms. One's cousin is the wing one flies with – could the bird fly without wings?"

D. Arab and Islamic Countries:
Article Twenty-Eight:

The Zionist invasion is a vicious invasion. It does not refrain from resorting to all methods, using all evil and contemptible ways to achieve its end. It relies greatly in its infiltration and espionage operations on the secret organizations it gave rise to, such as the Freemasons, The Rotary and Lions clubs, and other sabotage groups. All these organizations, whether secret or open, work in the interest of Zionism and according to its instructions. They aim at undermining societies, destroying values, corrupting consciences, deteriorating character and annihilating Islam. It is behind the drug trade and alcoholism in all its kinds so as to facilitate its control and expansion.

Arab countries surrounding Israel are asked to open their borders before the fighters from among the Arab and Islamic nations so that they could consolidate their efforts with those of their Muslim brethren in Palestine.

As for the other Arab and Islamic countries, they are asked to facilitate the movement of the fighters from and to it, and this is the least thing they could do.

We should not forget to remind every Muslim that when the Jews conquered the Holy City in 1967, they stood on the threshold of the Aqsa Mosque and proclaimed that "Mohammed is dead, and his descendants are all women."

Israel, Judaism and Jews challenge Islam and the Muslim people. "May the cowards never sleep."

E. Nationalist and Religious Groupings, Institutions, Intellectuals, The Arab and Islamic World:

The Islamic Resistance Movement hopes that all these groupings will side with it in all spheres, would support it, adopt its stand and solidify its activities and moves, work towards rallying support for it so that the Islamic people will be a base and a stay for it, supplying it with strategic depth an all human material and informative spheres, in time and in place. This should be done through the convening of solidarity conferences, the issuing of explanatory bulletins, favorable articles and booklets, enlightening the masses regarding the Palestinian issue, clarifying what confronts it and the conspiracies woven around it. They should mobilize the Islamic nations, ideologically, educationally and culturally, so that these peoples would be equipped to perform their role in the decisive battle of liberation, just as they did when they vanquished the Crusaders and the Tatars and saved human civilization. Indeed, that is not difficult for Allah.

"Allah hath written, Verily I will prevail, and my apostles: for Allah is strong and mighty." (The Dispute – verse 21).

Article Thirty:

Writers, intellectuals, media people, orators, educators and teachers, and all the various sectors in the Arab and Islamic world all of them are called upon to perform their role, and to fulfill their duty, because of the ferocity of the Zionist offensive and the Zionist influence in many countries exercised through financial and media control, as well as the consequences that all this lead to in the greater part of the world.

Jihad is not confined to the carrying of arms and the confrontation of the enemy. The effective word, the good article, the useful book, support and solidarity - together with the presence of sincere purpose for the hoisting of Allah's banner higher and higher all these are elements of the Jihad for Allah's sake.

"Whosoever mobilizes a fighter for the sake of Allah is himself a fighter. Whosoever supports the relatives of a fighter, he himself is a fighter." (related by al-Bukhari, Muslim, Abu-Dawood and al-Tarmadhi).

F. Followers of Other Religions: The Islamic Resistance Movement Is A Humanistic Movement:

Article Thirty-One:

The Islamic Resistance Movement is a humanistic movement. It takes care of human rights and is guided by Islamic tolerance when dealing with the followers of other religions. It does not antagonize anyone of them except if it is antagonized by it or stands in its way to hamper its moves and waste its efforts.

Under the wing of Islam, it is possible for the followers of the three religions - Islam, Christianity and Judaism to coexist in peace and quiet with each other. Peace and quiet would not be possible except under the wing of Islam. Past and present history are the best witness to that.

It is the duty of the followers of other religions to stop disputing the sovereignty of Islam in this region, because the day these followers should take over there will be nothing but carnage, displacement and terror. Every one of them is at variance with his fellow-religionists, not to speak about followers of other religionists. Past and present history are full of examples to prove this fact.

"They will not fight against you in a body, except in fenced towns, or from behind walls. Their strength in war among themselves is great: thou thinkest them to be united; but their hearts are divided. This, because they are people who do not understand." (The Emigration – verse 14).

Islam confers upon everyone his legitimate rights. Islam prevents the incursion on other people's rights. The Zionist Nazi activities against our people will not last for long. "For the state of injustice lasts but one day, while the state of justice lasts till Doomsday."

"As to those who have not borne arms against you on account of religion, nor turned you out of your dwellings, Allah forbiddeth you not to deal kindly with them, and to behave justly towards them; for Allah loveth those who act justly." (The Tried – verse 8).

The Attempt to Isolate the Palestinian People:

Article Thirty-Two:

World Zionism, together with imperialistic powers, try through a studied plan and an intelligent strategy to remove one Arab state after another from the circle of struggle against Zionism, in order to have it finally face the Palestinian people only. Egypt was, to a great extent, removed from the circle of the struggle, through the treacherous Camp David Agreement. They are trying to draw other Arab countries into similar agreements and to bring them outside the circle of struggle.

The Islamic Resistance Movement calls on Arab and Islamic nations to take up the line of serious and persevering action to prevent the success of this horrendous plan, to warn the people of the danger emanating from leaving the circle of struggle against Zionism. Today it is Palestine, tomorrow it will be one country or another. The Zionist plan is limitless. After Palestine, the Zionists aspire to expand from the Nile to the Euphrates. When they will have digested the region they overtook, they will aspire to further expansion, and so on. Their plan is embodied in the "Protocols of the Elders of Zion," and their present conduct is the best proof of what we are saying.

Leaving the circle of struggle with Zionism is high treason, and cursed be he who does that. "for whoso shall turn his back unto them on that day, unless he turneth aside to fight, or retreateth to another party of the faithful, shall draw on himself the indignation of Allah, and his abode shall be hell; an ill journey shall it be thither." (The Spoils – verse 16). There is no way out except by concentrating all powers and energies to face this Nazi, vicious Tatar invasion. The alternative is loss of one's country, the dispersion of citizens, the spread of vice on earth and the destruction of religious values. Let every person know that he is responsible before Allah, for "the doer of the slightest good deed is rewarded in like, and the doer of the slightest evil deed is also rewarded in like."

The Islamic Resistance Movement

consider itself to be the spearhead of the circle of struggle with world Zionism and a step on the road. The Movement adds its efforts to the efforts of all those who are active in the Palestinian arena. Arab and Islamic Peoples should augment by further steps on their part; Islamic groupings all over the Arab world should also do the same, since all of these are the best-equipped for the future role in the fight with the warmongering Jews.

"...and we have put enmity and hatred between them, until the day of resurrection. So often as they shall kindle a fire of war, Allah shall extinguish it; and they shall set their minds to act corruptly in the earth, but Allah loveth not the corrupt doers." (The Table – verse 64).

Article Thirty-Three:

The Islamic Resistance Movement, being based on the common coordinated and interdependent conceptions of the laws of the universe, and flowing in the stream of destiny in confronting and fighting the enemies in defense of the Muslims and

Islamic civilization and sacred sites, the first among which is the Aqsa Mosque, urges the Arab and Islamic peoples, their governments, popular and official groupings, to fear Allah where their view of the Islamic Resistance Movement and their dealings with it are concerned. They should back and support it, as Allah wants them to, extending to it more and more funds till Allah's purpose is achieved when ranks will close up, fighters join other fighters and masses everywhere in the Islamic world will come forward in response to the call of duty while loudly proclaiming: Hail to Jihad. Their cry will reach the heavens and will go on being resounded until liberation is achieved, the invaders vanquished and Allah's victory comes about.

"And Allah will certainly assist him who shall be on his side: for Allah is strong and mighty." (The Pilgrimage – verse 40).

The Testimony of History

Across History in Confronting the Invaders:

Article Thirty-Four:

Palestine is the navel of the globe and the crossroad of the continents. Since the dawn of history, it has been the target of expansionists. The Prophet, Allah bless him and grant him salvation, had himself pointed to this fact in the noble Hadith in which he called on his honorable companion, Ma'adh ben-Jabal, saying: O Ma'ath, Allah throw open before you, when I am gone, Syria, from Al-Arish to the Euphrates. Its men, women and slaves will stay firmly there till the Day of Judgement. Whoever of you should choose one of the Syrian shores, or the Holy Land, he will be in constant struggle till the Day of Judgement."

Expansionists have more than once put their eye on Palestine which they attacked with their armies to fulfill their designs on it. Thus it was that the Crusaders came with their armies, bringing with them their creed and carrying their Cross. They were able to defeat the Muslims for a while, but the Muslims were able to retrieve the land only when they stood under the wing of their *religious banner, united their word, hallowed the name of Allah and surged out fighting under the leadership of Salah ed-Din al-Ayyubi. They fought for almost twenty years and at the end the Crusaders were defeated and Palestine was liberated.*

"Say unto those who believe not, Ye shall be overcome, and thrown together into hell; an unhappy couch it shall be." (The Family of Imran – verse 12).

This is the only way to liberate Palestine. There is no doubt about the testimony of history. It is one of the laws of the universe and one of the rules of existence. Nothing can overcome iron except iron. Their false futile creed can only be defeated by the righteous Islamic creed. A creed could not be fought except by a creed, and in the last analysis, victory is for the just, for justice is certainly victorious.

"Our word hath formerly been given unto our servants the apostles; that they should certainly be assisted against the infidels, and that our armies should surely

be the conquerors." (Those Who Rank Themselves – verses 171172).

Article Thirty-Five:

The Islamic Resistance Movement views seriously the defeat of the Crusaders at the hands of Salah ed-Din al-Ayyubi and the rescuing of Palestine from their hands, as well as the defeat of the Tatars at Ein Galot, breaking their power at the hands of Qataz and Al-Dhaher Bivers and saving the Arab world from the Tatar onslaught which aimed at the destruction of every meaning of human civilization. The Movement draws lessons and examples from all this. The present Zionist onslaught has also been preceded by Crusading raids from the West and other Tatar raids from the East. Just as the Muslims faced those raids and planned fighting and defeating them, they should be able to confront the Zionist invasion and defeat it. This is indeed no problem for the Almighty Allah, provided that the intentions are pure, the determination is true and that Muslims have benefited from past experiences, rid themselves of the effects of ideological invasion and followed the customs of their ancestors.

The Islamic Resistance Movement is Composed of Soldiers:

Article Thirty-Six:

While paving its way, the Islamic Resistance Movement, emphasizes time and again to all the sons of our people, to the Arab and Islamic nations, that it does not seek personal fame, material gain, or social prominence. It does not aim to compete against any one from among our people, or take his place. Nothing of the sort at all. It will not act against any of the sons of Muslims or those who are peaceful towards it from among non-Muslims, be they here or anywhere else. It will only serve as a support for all groupings and organizations operating against the Zionist enemy and its lackeys.

The Islamic Resistance Movement adopts Islam as its way of life. Islam is its creed and religion. Whoever takes Islam as his way of life, be it an organization, a grouping, a country or any other body, the

Islamic Resistance Movement considers itself as their soldiers and nothing more.

We ask Allah to show us the right course, to make us an example to others and to judge between us and our people with truth. "O Lord, do thou judge between us and our nation with truth; for thou art the best judge." (Al Araf – Verse 89).

The last of our prayers will be praise to Allah, the Master of the Universe.

* * *

Political Islam and Nationalism in Hamas's Ideology:

Hamas's ideology is multifaceted, combining elements of religious fervor with the political struggle for Palestinian self-determination.

Hamas derives its principles from a strict interpretation of Islam, viewing the Quran and Sunnah as the ultimate guides for personal, political, and social life.

It believes in the establishment of an Islamic society governed by Sharia law.

The nationalist component of Hamas's

ideology is focused on the liberation of Palestine, which it regards as an Islamic right and duty, with armed struggle as a legitimate means.

Its nationalism is exclusionary, rejecting any form of Jewish sovereignty over what it considers to be Islamic lands.

Resistance and Jihad:

In the ideology of Hamas, the concepts of resistance and jihad are pivotal and interwoven with the very purpose of its existence. This can be understood in the context of their historical, political, and theological dimensions:

- **Historical Roots of Resistance:**
  Hamas positions itself in the lineage of past resistance movements against perceived foreign intrusion into Muslim lands. They draw parallels between their struggle and those of Muslims fighting against colonial or non-Muslim forces throughout history.

- **Political Jihad:** The group's concept of jihad extends beyond the physical confrontation with Israeli forces. It encompasses a broader political struggle against the state of Israel, aiming for the establishment of sovereignty over all of historic Palestine. This struggle is seen as both a defensive measure against occupation and an offensive to reclaim what they consider to be rightfully Palestinian and Islamic land.

- **Religious Mandate for Armed Struggle:** For Hamas, armed resistance is a divinely ordained duty. This interpretation of jihad as an armed struggle is rooted in their reading of Islamic texts, which they argue obligates Muslims to fight against the occupation of Islamic lands.

- **Tactics and Manifestations of Resistance:** Hamas's resistance takes multiple forms, from organized military activities of its armed wing, the Izz ad-Din al-Qassam Brigades, to inciting and supporting uprisings among the Palestinian population.

- **Impact on Peace Efforts:** Hamas's commitment to armed resistance is a significant obstacle to peace negotiations. Their attacks against Israeli targets have led to severe Israeli military responses and international condemnation, further complicating the peace process.
- **Social and Political Jihad:** Parallel to its military activities, Hamas engages in a 'social jihad' by providing social services and welfare to Palestinians, thus building a support base and legitimizing its governance role in Gaza.
- **International Implications:** The international community widely regards Hamas's armed activities as terrorism, leading to sanctions and a complex relationship with other states and international organizations.
- **Evolution of the Concept:** While the principle of armed struggle remains, Hamas has shown some political

pragmatism, as seen in ceasefires and political participation within the Palestinian Authority.

Resistance and jihad in the ideology of Hamas are both a practical strategy and a symbolic framework that underpins the group's identity and actions. It is a topic of intense debate and controversy, shaping not only Palestinian politics but also the broader dynamics of the Middle East conflict.

Hamas's ideology, while rooted in religious and historical narratives, has also shown some capacity for adaptation to political realities, as demonstrated by its participation in governance and elections within the Palestinian territories.

Chapter 4

The Founders

The following individuals were instrumental in establishing Hamas in 1987. Sheikh Ahmed Yassin and Abdel Aziz al-Rantissi, in particular, are often cited as the primary co-founders and were the most visible leaders until their deaths. Not all who founded are listed, below are considered very prominent.

* * *

Sheikh Ahmed Yassin:

Sheikh Ahmed Yassin was born in 1937 in Al-Jura, a village near Ashkelon, in what was then Mandatory Palestine. He became a quadriplegic at the age of 12 after sustaining a spinal cord injury while playing sports. Despite his disability, Yassin went on to become an important religious figure within the Palestinian community.

Yassin was a teacher and community leader in Gaza, deeply involved in Islamic charities and social activities. These activities laid the groundwork for what would later become Hamas. In 1987, amid the First

Courtesy of BBC

Intifada, Yassin co-founded Hamas as an offshoot of the Egyptian Muslim Brotherhood, advocating armed struggle against Israel.

Throughout his life, Yassin was seen as the spiritual leader of Hamas, guiding its policies and actions. He was arrested by Israel in 1989 for his role in orchestrating attacks against Israelis and was sentenced to life imprisonment. However, he was released in 1997 as part of a prisoner exchange.

Yassin continued to lead Hamas until his assassination in 2004 by an Israeli missile strike. His death did not diminish his status; he remains a revered figure for Hamas supporters, symbolizing resistance against Israeli occupation.

* * *

Abdel Aziz al-Rantisi:

Abdel Aziz al-Rantisi, a central figure in Palestinian politics and a co-founder of Hamas, was born on October 23, 1947, in the town of Yibna, near the historic port city of Jaffa. His life took a dramatic turn during the 1948 Arab-Israeli War when his family was compelled to relocate to the Gaza Strip, marking the beginning of a life under the shadow of conflict.

The violence of the conflict touched Rantisi personally at a young age. When he was just nine years old, his uncle was killed by Israeli soldiers in

Khan Younis, a formative event that profoundly influenced his worldview and political trajectory. These early experiences sowed the seeds of a deep-seated resistance against what he perceived as unjust occupation and aggression.

Rantisi was not only a political figure but also an accomplished academic. He pursued higher education with notable zeal and distinction, studying at Alexandria University in Egypt, where he specialized in pediatric medicine and genetics. His academic excellence was clear as he graduated first in his class, a testament to his intelligence and dedication. During his time in Egypt, Rantisi was drawn into the ideological orbit of the Muslim Brotherhood, a transnational Islamic movement, which would profoundly influence his political ideology and activities.

Returning to Gaza in 1976, Rantisi's career took a dual path: he was both an educator, imparting knowledge on parasitology and genetics at the Islamic University, and an emerging political activist. His commitment to the Palestinian cause and his intellectual background made him a respected figure in the eyes of many Palestinians.

Rantisi's rise as a political leader was marked

by the tumult of the First Intifada in 1987, a popular Palestinian uprising against Israeli rule. He stepped into the forefront as a key organizer, using his oratory and organizational skills to mobilize the masses in protest against the occupation. His efforts were crucial in the formation of Hamas, a movement that would become a central player in the Palestinian national movement.

However, his activism led to significant consequences; in December 1992, Rantisi, along with hundreds of other operatives, was deported to Lebanon. Despite the setback, he used this opportunity to become a vocal spokesman for the group, continuing to advocate for the Palestinian cause.

Tragedy struck when Rantisi was targeted and narrowly survived an Israeli helicopter attack in June 2003, an event that marked him as a prominent leader within the organization. Subsequently, after the assassination of Sheikh Ahmed Yassin in March 2004, Rantisi was named the leader of Hamas in the Gaza Strip. His tenure was characterized by fiery rhetoric and an uncompromising stance on the conflict with Israel.

He famously denounced the U.S. President George W. Bush and Israeli Prime Minister Ariel Sharon, aligning himself staunchly against Western policies in the region.

Rantisi's leadership, however, was short-lived. On April 17, 2004, he was assassinated in an Israeli Air Force strike, a move that sent shockwaves through the region and further solidified his status as a martyr in the eyes of his supporters. His life and death remain emblematic of the ongoing struggle and complexity of the Israeli-Palestinian conflict.

Hassan Yousef:

Hassan Yousef, a significant figure within Hamas, was born in the year 1955 in the city of Ramallah, at the time part of the Jordanian-administered West Bank. He emerged as one of the co-founders of Hamas, which is an Islamist political organization with a robust presence in both the Gaza Strip and the West Bank. His leadership role has been particularly noted in the West Bank.

In the eyes of many within Hamas, Yousef is seen as aligning with the organization's more hardline elements, and he is known for his staunch opposition to any form of reconciliation or peace talks with Israel. His ideological stance places him within the group of spiritual leaders who underscore Hamas's commitment to its foundational principles.

Yousef's personal life is marked by a significant familial legacy. He is married to Sabba Abu Salem, and together they have a sizeable family of six sons and three daughters. One of his sons, Mosab Hassan Yousef, has garnered attention for his collaboration with Israeli security service Shin Bet between 1997 and 2007, an involvement aimed at preventing attacks on Israeli targets. Mosab's actions, which he justified on moral grounds and in the interest of the Palestinian cause, led to his estrangement from his family, yet he is considered a hero by many in Israel and the United States.

In contrast, in 2019, Yousef's youngest son, Suheib, openly criticized Hamas, labeling it as corrupt and terroristic in an interview with Israeli television. This caused an uproar within Hamas, with accusations of betrayal and collaboration with Mossad, all of which Suheib denied.

Politically, Hassan Yousef's life has been punctuated by numerous arrests and periods of detention. His first arrest by Israeli authorities was in 1993, and he has since been detained multiple times, playing a prominent role during the Second Intifada. Yousef has spent more than two decades cumulatively in Israeli prisons, mostly under administrative detention, which is detention without formal charges or trial. His political involvements included a reluctant candidacy to represent Hamas in the 2005 elections while he was incarcerated, a candidacy he accepted under duress after learning of death threats to his eldest son.

His most recent arrests were part of an ongoing pattern, with the latest being part of a broader Israeli crackdown on Hamas activities. Hassan Yousef's life and actions have indelibly marked the history of Hamas and the broader Israeli-Palestinian conflict, reflecting the complex interplay between personal beliefs, political activism, and the tumultuous dynamics of the region.

Mahmoud Zahar:

Mahmoud al-Zahar, born on May 6, 1945, in Gaza City, is a co-founder of Hamas and has been a key leader within the organization, especially in the Gaza Strip. After graduating from Cairo University's Faculty of Medicine at 26, he later earned a master's degree in General Surgery from Ain Shams University. Al-Zahar was an adviser to the Palestinian Health Minister and helped establish the Islamic University in Gaza in 1978.

He played a significant role in founding Hamas in 1987. Following the assassination of Sheikh Ahmed Yassin, al-Zahar was rumored to have taken leadership of Hamas, but this was neither confirmed nor denied by the group, likely due to security concerns. He served as Foreign Minister in the Hamas-led Palestinian government in 2006 and has remained an influential figure within the movement.

* * *

Mohammad Taha:

Mohammad Taha was a Palestinian militant born in 1937 and passed away in November 2014. He was known as a co-founding member of Hamas. Taha was arrested by the Israel Defense Forces (IDF) in 2003 and held for 14 months without trial before being released back to Gaza in 2004. His son, Ayman Taha, was also involved with Hamas, serving as a spokesman and a former fighter. Mohammad Taha died after being hospitalized with a heart complaint.

Ibrahim al-Makadmeh:

Ibrahim al-Makadmeh, born in 1952, was a father of seven children and an influential figure within Hamas. His family was expelled from the village of Yibna, southwest of Jerusalem, and moved to refugee camps, settling finally in Jabalia. After studying dentistry in Egypt and adopting the Islamist ideology of the Muslim Brotherhood, he returned to Gaza and began organizing the Palestinian Islamist movement. Along with Sheikh Ahmed Yassin, he co-founded Hamas. He was arrested by the Israelis in 1984 for arms possession and was imprisoned for eight years, where he was allegedly tortured. Released in 1992, he worked as a dentist while continuing his activities with Hamas. He was critical of the Palestinian Authority and the Oslo Accords, which led to multiple arrests by Palestinian authorities. Al-Makadmeh was killed by Israeli forces in 2003.

These individuals played crucial roles in the formation and leadership of Hamas, deeply influencing the organization's direction and activities. Each had a significant impact on the development of the group and the broader Palestinian national movement.

Chapter 5

Hamas and the Palestine Liberation
Organization (PLO)

Hamas and the Palestine Liberation Organization (PLO) represent two distinct paradigms within Palestinian politics, each with its own history, ideological underpinnings, and vision for the Palestinian future.

I feel it's best to just simply detail them so you can easily compare. Many people are confused as both organizations seek an independent Palestinian State, but seek a sometimes divergent path.

Hamas:

- **Ideology:** Hamas is an Islamist movement that blends Palestinian nationalism with Islamic fundamentalism, drawing on the principles of the Muslim Brotherhood.
- **Formation and Activities:** Established during the First Intifada, it rapidly gained support for its social welfare programs and its stance against the Israeli occupation.
- **Governance:** After winning the 2006 Palestinian legislative elections, Hamas seized control of the Gaza Strip in 2007.
- **Military Tactics:** It has employed guerrilla tactics, suicide bombings, and rocket attacks against Israel, contributing to its designation as a terrorist organization by many nations.
- **Political Stance:** Hamas rejects the Oslo Accords and advocates for the establishment of an Islamic state over the entirety of historic Palestine, including the territory of current-day Israel.

* * *

Palestine Liberation Organization (PLO):

- **Origins:** Formed in 1964 with the goal of liberating Palestine, the PLO initially used guerrilla warfare and other forms of armed struggle against Israel.
- **International Recognition:** Recognized as the "sole legitimate representative of the Palestinian people," the PLO has sought to negotiate on behalf of Palestinians on the international stage.
- **Shift to Diplomacy:** Under the leadership of Yasser Arafat, the PLO shifted from armed struggle to diplomacy, culminating in the Oslo Accords, which established the Palestinian Authority (PA) and recognized the State of Israel.
- **Fatah's Role:** Fatah, the dominant party within the PLO led by Mahmoud Abbas, has pursued a two-state solution through negotiation and has been the face of the PA in the West Bank.

- **Current Challenges:** The PLO's influence has been challenged by the rise of Hamas, internal political divisions, and the stalled peace process.

Hamas vs. PLO Dynamics:

- **Rivalry:** The two entities have been at odds, with ideological and practical disputes over governance, resistance tactics, and the end goal for Palestinian statehood.
- **Conflict:** The rivalry erupted into a violent conflict in 2007 when Hamas ousted Fatah forces from Gaza, leading to a geographic and political split between the Gaza Strip and the West Bank.
- **Reconciliation Efforts:** There have been multiple attempts at reconciliation, with agreements signed but often not fully implemented, leaving the

Palestinian territories politically fragmented.

The split between Hamas and the PLO has complicated efforts to reach a peace agreement with Israel. Israel and other international actors have struggled to engage with a divided Palestinian leadership. The division has impacted the daily lives of Palestinians, with different administrations in the West Bank and Gaza Strip leading to varied experiences of governance, economic conditions, and freedoms.

The future of Hamas and the PLO, and their potential for reconciliation, remains a critical factor in the pursuit of a resolution to the Israeli-Palestinian conflict. The internal dynamics between these two factions, along with their relations with Israel and the broader international community, continue to shape the prospects for peace and the quest for Palestinian statehood.

Chapter 6

Governance and Social Services

Hamas's governance in the Gaza Strip encompasses a dual role of political leadership and provider of social services. Since taking control in 2007, Hamas has established a de facto administrative framework to govern the area, including setting up ministries and public institutions.

Governance:

Hamas operates as the primary governmental authority in Gaza, responsible for civil administration, public order, and policy implementation. It manages various sectors, including education, health, and infrastructure.

Hamas's governance in the Gaza Strip is characterized by its establishment of a parallel political system to the Palestinian Authority (PA). After winning the legislative elections in 2006 and the subsequent conflict with Fatah in 2007, Hamas set up its own administrative institutions in Gaza.

- **Government Structure:** Hamas formed a cabinet and appointed ministers to oversee various departments such as education, health, social affairs, and security. This government operates independently of the PA, which is based in the West Bank.
- **Security and Law Enforcement:** Hamas established its own security services, including a police force, border guards, and a military wing, the Izz ad-Din al-Qassam Brigades, which enforces its policies and maintains internal security.

- **Legal System:** The organization has implemented a legal system in Gaza that is influenced by Islamic law, which governs civil and criminal matters.
- **Economic Management:** Hamas controls the economy in the Gaza Strip, which is severely impacted by blockades and restrictions. It oversees the collection of taxes and the distribution of goods, and it attempts to facilitate trade under challenging circumstances.
- **Public Services:** Despite limited resources, Hamas attempts to provide public services such as healthcare, education, and infrastructure development, although these are often hampered by economic sanctions and the destruction caused by recurrent conflicts.
- **Challenges and Criticisms:** Hamas's governance has faced criticism for authoritarian practices, including suppression of dissent and restrictions on freedoms. It also struggles with international legitimacy, as many

governments do not recognize its rule over Gaza.

Overall, Hamas's governance involves managing the day-to-day administration of the Gaza Strip under conditions of isolation and conflict, striving to achieve its political objectives while dealing with internal and external challenges.

Social Services:

One of the pillars of Hamas's popularity is its network of social services. The organization has established clinics, schools, and charities, often stepping in to provide services where the official capacity is lacking. Hamas's extensive network of social services has played a significant role in its rise to power within the Gaza Strip.

- **Healthcare:** Hamas operates clinics and hospitals, providing medical services often at a low cost or free of charge, which is crucial in the impoverished and blockaded context of Gaza.

- **Education:** It has established schools that not only educate but also disseminate its political and religious ideologies.
- **Welfare Programs:** Hamas's welfare services offer support to the families of prisoners and those killed or wounded in conflicts, reinforcing loyalty and support among the populace.
- **Charitable Work:** Through various charities, Hamas assists in providing food, clothing, and shelter to the needy.

These services have contributed to Hamas's popularity and influence, as they are seen as stepping in where the Palestinian Authority and international aid have been insufficient. However, its role as a service provider is intertwined with its political and military activities, which affects the international community's willingness to engage with and support these social programs.

* * *

Challenges:

Hamas faces significant challenges in governance, including economic sanctions, border blockades, military conflicts with Israel, and internal political pressures.

Internationally, Hamas's governance is not officially recognized by many states, and it is seen as a terrorist organization by several countries, impacting its ability to engage in formal diplomacy and receive foreign aid.

Hamas's role in Gaza continues to be a subject of significant political debate and has major implications for Israeli-Palestinian relations and the broader Middle East peace process.

Chapter 7

The Military Dimension

The Izz ad-Din al-Qassam Brigades:

The Izz ad-Din al-Qassam Brigades is the military wing of Hamas and is named after Izz ad-Din al-Qassam, a Palestinian nationalist leader and Islamic preacher who fought against British and Zionist forces in the early 20th century. The Brigades were formed in the early 1990s, evolving from the violent uprisings of the First Intifada into a structured militant group.

* * *

Operations and Tactics:

The Qassam Brigades conduct a range of military operations including:

- Rocket attacks into Israeli territory.
- Suicide bombings, particularly during the Second Intifada.
- Tunneling operations for smuggling and infiltration.
- Kidnappings.

The Brigades have a hierarchical command structure but also operate with a degree of autonomy at the local level, allowing for cells to plan and execute operations independently.

Their funding comes from various sources, including Iran, private donations, and illicit activities. The group has developed domestic rocket production capabilities and uses a variety of weapons smuggled through tunnels from Egypt.

In Gaza, the Qassam Brigades are both revered and feared. They are seen as defenders of Palestinian rights by many but are also criticized for their role in the ongoing conflict with Israel and the resultant civilian casualties and economic hardships.

Many countries, including Israel, the United States, and members of the European Union, have designated the Qassam Brigades as a terrorist organization due to their tactics and targeting of civilians.

The presence and actions of the Qassam Brigades have a significant impact on the Israeli-Palestinian conflict with the Izz ad-Din al-Qassam Brigades play a central role in Hamas's strategy of resistance and have been a key factor in the group's resilience and political power within Gaza. Their actions continue to shape the security situation in the region and the dynamics of the Palestinian political landscape.

Chapter 8

Internal Conflicts and Governance

Hamas and Fatah:

The split between Hamas and Fatah is a defining moment in Palestinian politics, leading to a geographic and political division that persists to this day.

Hamas and Fatah have long held different visions for Palestinian governance and statehood. Fatah, the leading party within the PLO, has historically supported a two-state solution and engaged in peace negotiations with Israel. Hamas, on the other hand, emerged with an Islamist ideology, advocating armed resistance and refusing to recognize Israel.

* * *

2006 Elections and Aftermath:

The 2006 Palestinian legislative elections were a watershed moment in modern Middle Eastern politics. Occurring on January 25, 2006, these elections saw the Islamist group Hamas win a decisive victory over the long-dominant Fatah party.

Pre-Election Context:

- The elections were the first in the Palestinian territories since 1996 and were seen as a key step in the democratic process post-Oslo Accords.

- Fatah, the party of Yasser Arafat, was marred by internal divisions and allegations of corruption, diminishing its public support.

Election Results:

- Hamas won 74 of the 132 seats in the Palestinian Legislative Council, whereas Fatah won just 45. This outcome was unexpected by many international observers.

Immediate Aftermath:

- The victory of Hamas, designated as a terrorist organization by many countries, led to a reassessment of international aid and engagement with the Palestinian Authority.

- Economic sanctions and a withholding of aid by Western countries followed, severely impacting the Palestinian economy.

Fatah-Hamas Conflict:

The Fatah-Hamas conflict escalated dramatically following the 2006 Palestinian legislative elections. The competition for control of the Palestinian Authority (PA) turned violent as both parties sought to assert their authority.

Clashes between Fatah and Hamas militants intensified, leading to numerous fatalities and injuries.

In June 2007, Hamas militants took control of the Gaza Strip after a series of battles with Fatah forces, effectively splitting the governance of the Palestinian territories.

The Palestinian Authority split into two

separate administrations: a Hamas-led administration in Gaza and a Fatah-led administration in the West Bank.

The international community largely backed the Fatah-led PA in the West Bank, while Hamas faced economic sanctions and political isolation in Gaza.

Various attempts at reconciliation, including multiple rounds of talks and agreements brokered by other countries, have taken place but have failed to produce a lasting unity government.

This division has had a profound effect on the politics, economy, and social conditions in the Palestinian territories, contributing to the complexity of the Israeli-Palestinian conflict.

The split resulted in two separate Palestinian governments, with Hamas ruling Gaza and the Palestinian Authority controlling parts of the West Bank.

Repeated attempts at reconciliation have been made but with limited success, affecting the peace process and the stability of the region.

Chapter 9

Perspectives

Views From the Palestinian Society:

From the Palestinian perspective, views on Hamas are complex and multifaceted, influenced by political, social, and religious factors. For some Palestinians, Hamas is seen as a legitimate resistance movement fighting against Israeli occupation and for Palestinian self-determination. They point to Hamas's social welfare programs, which provide much-needed services in the impoverished regions of the Gaza Strip, as evidence of its commitment to the Palestinian people.

However, other Palestinians criticize Hamas for its governance of the Gaza Strip, citing issues such as human rights abuses, suppression of dissent, and the negative impact of its military actions on the civilian population. The international isolation and economic sanctions that have followed Hamas's control of Gaza have also been a point of contention, with some Palestinians feeling that these policies have worsened living conditions and hindered the quest for statehood.

These contrasting views within the Palestinian society reflect the broader debate over the effectiveness of Hamas's strategies and its role in the future of the Palestinian cause.

Perspectives From the International Community:

The international community's perspective on Hamas is divided but largely critical due to its designation as a terrorist organization by many countries, including Israel, the United States, the European Union, Canada, and Japan. This designation is primarily due to Hamas's use of suicide bombings, rocket attacks against Israeli civilians, and its charter that calls for the destruction of Israel.

Conversely, some nations and organizations, particularly in the Middle East and among Islamic countries, view Hamas as a legitimate resistance movement fighting Israeli occupation. The group has political support and has received financial aid from countries like Iran.

The conflicting views on Hamas are reflective of the broader complexities of the Middle East conflict, where geopolitics, historical grievances, and ideological divides play significant roles. The international response to Hamas involves a mix of diplomatic isolation, economic sanctions, and, at times, dialogue—though any engagement is often contingent on the group's stance towards violence and recognition of Israel.

Chapter 10

October 7, 2023 and Beyond

On October 7, 2023, the morning following the 50th anniversary of the 1973 Yom Kippur War, Hamas executed an unexpected offensive against Israel. This attack involved both an incursion by armed militants across defensive perimeters and a volley of rockets launched from the Gaza Strip, coinciding with the Jewish celebration of Simchat Torah.

The following is a timeline of events:

Early in the morning, around 6:30 am local time (03:30 GMT), Hamas launched a significant rocket assault on southern Israel, triggering alarms as distant as Tel

Aviv and Beersheba. According to Hamas, the initial salvo consisted of 5,000 rockets, while the Israeli military reported that 2,500 rockets were fired. The attack caused plumes of smoke to rise from Israeli residential areas as citizens sought cover, with reports of at least one fatality resulting from the rockets. Mohammed Deif, the leader of Hamas's military wing, proclaimed the onset of "Operation Al-Aqsa Flood," stating that the first strike targeting Israeli military sites involved over 5,000 missiles and shells.

At 7:40 am (04:40 GMT), amid a barrage of rocket fire, the Israeli military reported that Palestinian militants had infiltrated Israel's borders. The majority exploited gaps in the security fences that demarcate the boundaries between Gaza and Israel. Notably, one Hamas militant was recorded using a powered parachute to cross over, while a motorboat carrying combatants was spotted heading towards Zikim, home to an Israeli coastal town and military installation. Visual evidence of the breach included footage of fighters on at least six motorcycles passing through an opening in a metal fence and an image disseminated by Hamas of a bulldozer demolishing a section of the barrier.

At 9:45 am local time (06:45 GMT), explosions resounded throughout Gaza. Shortly thereafter, at 10:00 am (07:00 GMT), the spokesperson for the Israeli military confirmed that the air force had commenced operations targeting locations within the Gaza Strip.

By 10 am local time (07:00 GMT), Israeli military sources reported that Palestinian militants had infiltrated several military sites along the border area. These included the Beit Hanoon (Erez) crossing, the Zikim military base, and the Gaza division's headquarters at Reim. Videos released by Hamas depicted militants advancing towards and setting ablaze a structure adjacent to a tall concrete barrier with a watchtower, as well as what appeared to be militants taking control of parts of an Israeli military installation. Saleh al-Arouri,

Hamas's deputy chief in the West Bank, publicly urged a wider engagement in the conflict. Images later circulated showing Israeli military vehicles seized during the fighting being displayed in Gaza.

Militants launched assaults on multiple Israeli locations including the town of Sderot, the community of Be'eri, and Ofakim, situated around 30 kilometers east of the Gaza Strip, as per reports from Israeli outlets. Southern Israeli residents have been reinforcing their homes to serve as bomb shelters, utilizing them as safe rooms amidst the conflict. The Israeli military has instructed citizens to remain indoors, broadcasting messages of imminent support. Into the night, Israeli forces were engaged in efforts to secure areas that had seen incursions by Hamas militants.

Israeli reports detailed incidents of hostage-taking in the town of Ofakim. Claims from Palestinian Islamic Jihad mentioned the capture of Israeli soldiers. Social media channels associated with

Hamas circulated videos purporting to show captives being escorted into Gaza. Footage displayed three individuals, casually dressed in vests, shorts, and flip-flops, being led through a facility marked with Hebrew script. Additional videos appeared to show the capture of female individuals and Israeli soldiers being forcibly removed from a military vehicle.

The head of the Palestinian Islamic Jihad announced that in the wake of Saturday's offensive, the group had detained over 30 Israelis in Gaza. He stipulated that these captives would only be set free in exchange for the release of all Palestinians currently incarcerated in Israeli prisons.

Into the late hours of Saturday night, Israeli forces sustained their aerial bombardments while rockets continued to be launched into southern Israel. Israeli military personnel were engaged with Hamas militants across 22 different sites in proximity to the Gaza border, indicating the extensive scale of the conflict. The Israeli military reported ongoing combat with "hundreds" of Palestinian fighters who had entered Israeli territory.

On Sunday, October 8, Israeli Prime Minister announced that Israel had formally declared war against Hamas.

As of the printing of this book, the war still rages in Gaza.

What Prompted the Attack?:

Hamas leaders pointed to ongoing grievances that ignited the recent attack. They noted the tensions around the Al-Aqsa Mosque/Temple Mount, a site revered in both Islam and Judaism. Clashes at this holy site, including the conflict in 2021, have been flashpoints in the past. Israeli nationalists' increased presence at the compound, especially during recent Jewish festivals, has been met with strong criticism from Hamas. Additionally, the expansion of Jewish settlements, tougher conditions for Palestinian inmates, and violent border protests have fueled discontent. Hamas has been seeking concessions to alleviate Gaza's blockade and economic woes, with an eye on the wider regional dynamics, including Israel's potential normalization of ties with Saudi Arabia, which have predominantly addressed West Bank issues, not Gaza's concerns.

* * *

Shifting Perspectives:

Globally, the perspective on Hamas is diverse and reflects varying geopolitical interests and policy stances:

- **Support for Israel:** Many nations, particularly in the West, including the United States and several European countries, unequivocally condemn Hamas's militant actions and support Israel's right to self-defense.
- **Advocacy for Peace:** A segment of the international community is vocal about the need for de-escalation, advocating for an end to violence and the resumption of peace negotiations. This has resulted in widespread protests for

ceasefire around the world and many capital cities.

- **Separating Hamas from the Palestinian People:** A clear line is drawn by some international actors between the deeds of Hamas and the broader Palestinian society, stressing the importance of not attributing the group's actions to all Palestinians.
- **Terrorist Designation by the U.S.:** The United States officially classifies Hamas as a foreign terrorist organization, influencing its policies and actions towards the group.
- **Attention to the Incursion:** The scale of Hamas's incursion in southern Israel has captured international attention, with the timing coinciding with Israel's internal political turmoil, adding to the complexity of the situation.
- **Human Cost:** The death toll and hostage-taking in the recent attacks have subjected Hamas to rigorous international scrutiny.

The international viewpoint on Hamas, therefore, involves both disapproval of its violent methods and concerns for the stability of the region, coupled with calls for discerning the group's actions from the general Palestinian struggle for statehood. The conflict's intricacies and the significant loss of life during such conflicts are central in informing the international dialogue on Hamas and the ongoing Israeli-Palestinian peace process.

Conclusion

In conclusion, the story of Hamas and its role within the Palestinian-Israeli conflict is a complex narrative woven through decades of historical grievances, ideological clashes, and the relentless pursuit of sovereignty and survival. This book has sought to provide a comprehensive exploration of Hamas's evolution from a local Islamist movement to a significant political and military force within the Palestinian territories and a central player on the international stage.

The trajectory of Hamas is marked by its social welfare programs that endeared it to the Palestinian population, its political ascendancy challenged by international sanctions and regional politics, and its militant resistance against Israel, which has drawn condemnation and conflict. The group's actions, particularly the audacious attacks of October 7, 2023, have not only reshaped the geopolitical discourse but have also rekindled debates about the strategies, aspirations, and future of the Palestinian cause.

The international community's response to Hamas oscillates between outright condemnation and a nuanced understanding that distinguishes between the actions of the organization and the broader Palestinian struggle for self-determination. The West, led by the United States, remains firm in its denunciation of Hamas's tactics, while other global actors call for a more balanced approach that recognizes the complex realities of life under occupation and the right to resist.

The split between Hamas and Fatah reflects the internal fragmentation of Palestinian politics, further complicating the path to statehood and peace. The repercussions of this division are felt not just in the diplomatic arenas but also in the everyday lives of Palestinians, who navigate the realities of governance by two separate administrations.

The future of Hamas and its impact on the Palestinian-Israeli conflict remains uncertain. As regional dynamics shift and global powers reassess their roles in the Middle East, the potential for significant change looms. Yet, the fundamental issues at the heart of Hamas's creation and continued existence—the occupation, the blockade of Gaza, and the right to self-determination—persist.

In the final analysis, the story of Hamas is intrinsically linked to the enduring quest for a resolution to the Israeli-Palestinian conflict—a quest that is as much about the search for peace as it is about the unyielding demand for dignity and justice. As the region looks towards an uncertain future, the legacy of Hamas's actions, the international community's response, and the unfulfilled aspirations of the Palestinian people will undoubtedly continue to shape the discourse and outcomes of this historic conflict.

About the Author

Tariq Nassar is a Palestinian researcher based in the United States, currently engaged in graduate studies at a prominent university. His academic journey began in the shadowed alleys of historic Jerusalem, where the complex interplay of history and modern strife fueled his passion for Middle Eastern politics. *Between Faith and Fury: The Story of Hamas* represents Nassar's first foray into the literary world, offering a meticulous account of the organization's influence on the Israeli-Palestinian discourse, shaped by both his heritage and his scholarly endeavors in the U.S.